55 Antique Skyscrapers
& the
Business Tycoons Who Built Them

Mark Houser

Cover illustration by Cricket Houser

First edition

ISBN: 978-0-578-80736-2

This book was professionally typeset on Reedsy.
Find out more at reedsy.com

To Elaine, my mother, who always encouraged me to look up

We defy you even to aspire to venerate shapes so grossly constructed as the arrangement in fifty floors. You may have a feeling for keeping on with an old staircase, consecrated by the tread of generations—especially when it's "good," and old staircases are often so lovely; but how can you have a feeling for keeping on with an old elevator, how can you have it any more than for keeping on with an old omnibus?

– Henry James

Contents

1

A Brief History of Building High

The title of world's tallest skyscraper is only ever a temporary distinction. The Empire State Building held the honor for forty years, longer than any other skyscraper has, but half a century has passed since it surrendered the accolade. Its fifth successor, the Burj Khalifa in Dubai, seized the mantle of loftiest building upon its completion in 2009.

Think back to when you first saw it. You were probably at least a little bit amazed. Certainly it helped if you saw Tom Cruise sprint across the side of it while dangling from a cable in *Mission: Impossible—Ghost Protocol*. At 2,717 feet, the Burj Khalifa is almost twice the height of the Sears Tower, whose 1,450 feet set the world record when it opened in 1974.

Now take that three-and-a-half-decade timespan that it took to go from Sears Tower to Burj Khalifa and roll it back to a century earlier. Thirty-four years passed from the day the good citizens of New York City beheld the world's first ten-story office building—the Western Union Building of 1875—until the day they had to reconcile their minds with the world's first fifty-story skyscraper, the 1909 Metropolitan Life Tower. Mercifully, Tom Cruise was not around yet, or their heads might have exploded.

Skyscrapers are approaching their sesquicentennial anniversary. For nearly a century and a half they have stood as archetypes of technology and progress, symbolizing and manifesting the aspirations of humankind. But if we look today at the very first skyscrapers, now dwarfed by giants and dressed up like

Greek temples from antiquity, we may find it hard to conceive that these too were once seen as modern marvels.

A ten-story building, after all, is hardly a remarkable sight to you or me or anyone now. But try to imagine that you have lived your whole life without ever seeing one. The main streets of your city have always been lined with stores and offices and hotels and apartments that are five stories tall at most. The reason is straightforward: Five stories is as far as anyone realistically can be expected to climb a staircase.

An 1874 illustration of New York before skyscrapers shows the near-uniform height of buildings interrupted by a few church steeples. (The artist shows the Brooklyn Bridge complete, although it was then under construction.)

Now imagine that suddenly the first ten-story building you have ever seen sprouts up from the sidewalk to soar above the others. Immediately, its neighbors on the block are overshadowed and under threat. More towers quickly follow in its wake, until the neat horizontal border of five-story rooflines you have known since childhood begins to resemble a lawn overrun by dandelions. And the dandelions keep getting taller.

Keep in mind also that, unlike now, when we have a mental framework for newer and taller skyscrapers, people in those days never had seen anything like one. It was a widespread fear that such precarious contraptions would surely blow over in the first strong gust. The architect of one of New York's first skyscrapers, the Tower Building, actually clambered to the top of his unfinished eleven-story structure in the middle of a violent storm, and as crowds gathered at a safe distance to see if the building swayed or tumbled in gale force winds reaching seventy miles per hour, he dropped a plumb line. It didn't budge.

Safety concerns went beyond wind bracing. Early skyscrapers had to be equipped with adequate safeguards against fire, as well as reliable escape routes for any inhabitants unlucky enough to be caught inside in the event the fireproofing failed. A panoply of other technical challenges had to be surmounted, including ventilation, heat, light, plumbing, and adequate elevator service.

Once those were addressed to general satisfaction, tall office construction projects blossomed, first in New York and Chicago, and soon across the country. Searching for a descriptive term to encompass these awe-inspiring additions to the downtown grid, newspapers adopted a word already familiar to readers. In different contexts it could describe a racehorse, a bonnet, a preacher, an astronomer, or a sail at the top of a ship's mast. But its most widespread usage by then was in stories about the popular new sport of baseball, where it described a high fly ball: a sky-scraper.

The novelist Henry James, returning in 1904 to New York City after a twenty-one-year sojourn in Europe, was stunned by the colossal interlopers he found looming over the city of his birth. These "monsters of the mere market," he wrote in *Harper's Weekly*, were "like extravagant pins in a cushion already overplanted, and stuck in as in the dark, anywhere and anyhow."

Other critics claimed tall buildings would swamp the real estate market, cause overcrowding and disease, and blot out the sunlight. To win over the public, those who constructed the first high-rises employed features engineered for mass appeal. Many had observation decks, and some even maintained rooftop gardens where patrons could gather for alfresco dining, concerts, and theatrical performances. At street level, no expense was spared on extravagant lobbies, making liberal use of Italian marble, rich wood paneling, and elaborate brass fixtures and accents.

Lower Manhattan skyline from the Hudson in 1913

Draftsmen employed design motifs and decorative elements from ancient Greek and Roman architecture to convey an air of sophistication and class. Many prominent architects of the era had studied in Paris at the influential École des Beaux-Arts (School of Fine Arts), and the school lent its name to a neoclassical style of ornamentation that became highly fashionable: Beaux-Arts (pronounced "*boze ar*"). Not only were facades primped with columns in the Doric, Ionic, or Corinthian orders, but the buildings themselves were designed deliberately to resemble a classical Greek column. The typical antique skyscraper incorporates a base for the entrance and shops that is robed in a heavy stone, often granite. That is surmounted by a shaft of offices with a complementary cladding, either of brick or terracotta. Finally it is topped with elaborate decorations on the uppermost floors, constituting the column's capital.

Such outer trappings of high culture helped to mask the structure's true purpose: facilitating commerce. As companies grew, so did their need for accounting, recordkeeping, correspondence, and other clerical work. This required trained professional staff, ideally in one centralized location. All those white-collar workers congregating in ever-increasing numbers helped to drive up the value of downtown real estate. Landowners looking to maximize the value of their parcels saw that stacking floors upon floors multiplied the number of leaseholders whom they could charge rent.

Skyscrapers also enabled another attractive convenience. Firms that did business together could share a building. It was so much easier to hammer out the details of a contract or deal if, rather than sending a telegram or a messenger boy across town, the principals were just a short elevator ride away.

"A machine that makes the land pay" is how Cass Gilbert distilled the essence of a skyscraper in a 1900 essay. Gilbert was one of the most acclaimed early skyscraper architects, well aware of the complicated marriage of art and engineering required to produce some colossal new edifice for a paying client. He also fundamentally understood what impelled that client to seek him out in the first place, the source of the demand that ultimately rewarded architects such as himself with considerable fame and bountiful fees: the profit motive. Namely, who could design the most appealing office block and woo the most lucrative tenants?

* * *

America at the end of the nineteenth century was a testing ground of unfettered capitalism. It was also an age of full-scale societal disruption driven by technological advances that struck like lightning. Transcontinental railroads. Gargantuan factories. Instantaneous communication via telegraph, telephone, and undersea cable. New sources of energy—oil, natural gas, and electricity—to power the country's industrialization and fuel new modes of transport. By the 1920s, automobiles would crowd horse-drawn carriages off the roads, and even the skies would be conquered by flying machines. And, of course, by skyscrapers.

Behind each new skyscraper construction project was an investor. Almost always, it was someone who had made a reputation and a fortune through some novel product or business insight, through some innovation in manu-facturing or marketing or retail. Or someone who, by perception and instinct, by know-how and guts, had risen through the ranks of the organization to a powerful perch.

Now this man—only in extremely rare circumstances was it a woman—had two urges he wished to satisfy: first, to earn further returns on his wealth, and second, to do so while gaining the kind of stature and notoriety that might come from having a skyscraper of one's own.

This book is a collection of those stories. Who were these tycoons, these businessmen and capitalists and entrepreneurs who had the money and the desire to build their cities' first skyscrapers?

They came from practically every field of endeavor. Banking and investment. Insurance and law. Manufacturing across the spectrum—pharmaceuticals and soft drinks, automobiles and typewriters, bathtubs and steel rails. They were powerful government officials, luxury hotel owners, and Hollywood promoters. Oil barons, railroad barons, retail barons, and mass media barons. Most were wealthy, but the people who commissioned skyscrapers were not idle rich. Many came from humble origins, and a few even tumbled back.

Were they robber barons? Some certainly relied on business practices that would not be tolerated today. Their stories reveal much about the society of their time, including its deep flaws. Few women during that era had the means and influence to commission a tall office building. Most gay people were essentially forced to hide that part of their identity, so their stories sometimes involve a degree of conjecture. Unfortunately, but not surprisingly, research for this work could not locate a single example of an early skyscraper built for an African American. Nevertheless, this book includes the stories of several Black people who played important parts in the history of these buildings.

Some of the innovations that generated fortunes for these tycoons may seem unimpressive to us at first. One family dynasty was built on shovels. Another emerged from an empire of five-and-dime stores. But before we make any definitive judgements, we should imagine what people a century and more from today will think of our own technology. Perhaps, we can always hope, they will be too polite to laugh out loud.

The stories in this book are about people who transformed society in ways that are still felt today. With their successes and with their failures, they laid the groundwork for industries and business practices of our modern world. They are yesteryear's iteration of the Silicon Valley computer geeks who tinkered in their garages to create Apple and Google.

By and large, their stories have long been forgotten. But through the skyscrapers they built, these people played a part in transforming their cities. They left a legacy, one that might be sifted for insight about our present concerns. In the end, it might fairly be said, they succeeded.

To be clear: Architects conceived and designed these first skyscrapers. They were the indispensable creative force; without them, none of these buildings would exist. But before any architect took on a skyscraper project, he first had to be commissioned by somebody who wanted a skyscraper built.

It would be a mistake to assume their collaboration ended with the commission. Why wouldn't these wealthy and powerful customers have certain ideas about how their building should look? They had seen other skyscrapers. Many had visited the great buildings of Europe during a transatlantic tour. Surely they had strong opinions about what they liked and didn't like, and they hadn't gotten rich by being shy. Their instructions to the architects had an important impact on the finished products; in some cases they propelled visionary achievements. For instance, take a pair of famous Chicago skyscrapers described in this book, the Monadnock and Reliance buildings. Both owe their most crucial architectural innovation—the former its sober, slab-like aspect, the latter its gleaming half-acre of windowpanes—to meeting the specific demands of the moneymen.

Early skyscrapers were purely American. The form, which originated in Chicago and New York, could be found in every large American city—and for the most part, nowhere else. The long-established capitals of Europe certainly possessed the means to build skyscrapers had they so desired. But their city centers already were loaded with fine architectural ensembles, and residents had little desire to demolish those. They also were curtailed by building height limits far more restrictive than any in the United States. Even the strictest U.S. height limits—110 feet in Washington, D.C., and 125 feet in Boston—allowed more altitude than standard European maximums, such as 80 feet in London and 20 meters (about 65 feet) in Paris.

Of course, the Eiffel Tower was a significant exception. At just under one thousand feet, the iconic assemblage of iron beams outstripped anything built on this planet for forty years. Intended as a temporary showpiece for the 1889 World's Fair, the tower so enchanted Parisians that they allowed it to remain. While not a skyscraper—that categorization requires, at a bare minimum, walls—the Eiffel Tower was erected using the same kind of metal framework that made skyscrapers possible.

Nor were skyscrapers the first tall structures. People have been climbing the stairs of the eleven-story Liaodi Pagoda in China for almost a thousand years; at 276 feet tall, the Buddhist tower of stone and brick tops out higher than several buildings in this book. However, it was not constructed for continual habitation and use, as skyscrapers are, but rather as a watchtower and storage facility for sacred texts. Similarly, the steeples of some medieval cathedrals exceed the height of early skyscrapers, but their only steady occupants are bats, not businessmen.

Indeed, the steeple of Trinity Church was the highest point in New York for most of the nineteenth century. Visitors could ascend its spiral stairs for panoramic views up and down Broadway. It yielded the honor for a brief period when the city held its 1853 World's Fair, which featured a 315-foot-tall timber observation tower. Hardy sightseers could climb its staircase until they were looking down on the spire at Trinity—at least until 1855, when new owners removed the tower's top section. (The rest of it burned down the following year.)

A more consequential exhibit at the first American world's fair was that of Elisha Otis, who demonstrated his elevator safety brake. The inventor and former wagonmaker hoisted himself fifty feet up on a loaded freight elevator, and then, as spectators gasped, cut the rope. His brake system prevented a fatal plunge, and before the decade was out, Otis's company would install the world's first successful passenger elevator in a New York department store.

The transformative decade for lofty construction projects came in the 1880s. The Washington Monument broke the world height record in 1884, the Statue of Liberty rose in New York harbor two years after that, and finally, the same French engineer who had devised an iron framework to support the statue's copper skin unveiled his astonishing tower in Paris in 1889. The decade also saw the first skyscrapers borne by metal skeletons like the one holding up Lady Liberty, rather than by massive load-bearing masonry walls of stone or brick, as all tall buildings had been before.

The extraordinarily popular Chicago World's Fair of 1893 cemented a gathering trend of monumentalism, of marrying architectural elements from the old world with the soaring structures of the new. It spawned a movement called City Beautiful, which propounded that the "huddled masses yearning to breathe free" pouring into America's cities could be inculcated with the values of public citizenship and democracy if they were surrounded by dignified buildings.

An 1894 issue of Scientific American compares the magazine's headquarters (at left) with Chicago's tallest skyscraper, the Masonic Temple (demolished in 1939); New York's Trinity Church; the Statue of Liberty; the U.S. Capitol; and the Ferris Wheel at the Chicago World's Fair.

Skyscrapers continued to spread and multiply. By 1929, America had more than five thousand buildings of ten stories or more.

But by then, backward-looking Beaux-Arts was no longer the architectural mode of choice. It had been supplanted by a modernist decorative aesthetic known as Art Deco. Characterized by streamlined curves and bold angles, highlighted with bright colors and chrome, it celebrated and tried to mimic the latest technological enhancements in locomotives and airplanes. As if to place an exclamation point on this bold new era of industrial design, in 1929 the burnished spire of the Chrysler Building, the literal pinnacle of Art Deco skyscrapers, shot past the Eiffel Tower to take the laurels for tallest structure in the world. It would enjoy that distinction for almost a year, until another Art Deco skyscraper, the Empire State Building, surpassed it.

Now hopelessly unfashionable, the old skyscrapers—with their cramped offices, slow elevators, fire code violations, and lack of air conditioning—were wanted no more. Over the years, many were demolished to make way for new developments. Those that survived were remodeled or modernized, some so drastically as to render them unrecognizable. An excellent example is the 1904 New York Times Building, which gave Times Square its name. The owners replaced its exterior with a white marble and glass shell in the 1960s, but even that so-called improvement is barely visible anymore now that the building is practically buried under enormous electronic signs.

A few of the original skyscrapers managed to hang on. Although musty and neglected, in the end some simply were too pretty to demolish. Many owe their survival to preservationists, advocates who battled back against the bulldozers until the structures were seen as valuable pieces of cultural heritage and protected as such. Others were just lucky.

That is the scope of this book. Across thirty-six cities, it compiles a collection of these venerable high-rises and tells the stories of the businessmen who brought them into being. Many have been restored to their former glory, often for luxury apartments or boutique hotels. You can see them with your own eyes and stroll through their often stupendous lobbies, and imagine an earlier time when they were the tallest thing around. These were legitimate tourist attractions. People bought souvenir postcards of them (the same vintage postcards that illustrate this book) and mailed them to the folks back home: Wish you were here, and would you look at this!

When you visit these antique skyscrapers, give a thought to the proud people who created them: the laborers who risked their lives teetering on crossbeams high above the sidewalk, the immigrants who drove the mule teams hauling gigantic steel girders in the days before tractor trailers, the engineers and contractors and plumbers, the architects who sketched and crumpled and sketched until a concept was ready to be transformed into reality.

Especially, think of the founders, the strivers and the men of means, the entrepreneurs and the powers that were, who looked at a plot of urban land and thought: That's where I build my legacy.

* * *

The skyscrapers selected for these pages cover a four-decade span, from 1889 to 1928. They meet three criteria:

- They are at least ten stories tall.
- They still exist, so you can see them now.
- They are decorated in a pre-modern style.

Beyond those three criteria, and the occasional pertinent or especially interesting background detail, this book does not employ specialized architectural terminology, nor does it concern itself with weighty considerations of artistic merit. The author claims no expertise in that regard. Any building in this book is included simply because, in the author's opinion, it looks cool.

Buildings typically outlast their builders. When they change hands, they sometimes change names. This book refers to buildings as they were known on the day they opened. Even with new names, they remain easy to find. Downtowns a century ago were far more compact than now. Readers are encouraged to seek out these buildings and have a look for themselves. Walk on in. It is possible to enter most of them without special arrangement, and it is almost always worth the trouble.

Most books about antique skyscrapers focus on New York and Chicago. That is understandable, since they are the birthplace of skyscrapers. This book aims for a broader reach. It starts with four buildings in each of those cities in order to establish a context, but then it moves on to spend most of its pages in the rest of the United States. Historic high-rises in most of America's major cities are grouped in four additional chapters—Northeast, Midwest, South, and West—for a total of fifty U.S. skyscrapers, a nice round American number.

There are also five bonus international entries, showing how the tall building trend began its spread across the globe. Two are in Canada, two are in Europe, and one is in South America.

None are in the Middle East or Asia. While those locales are without question the current epicenters of awe-inducing construction, they offer scant examples of antique skyscrapers. One impressive Asian building of the period, a twelve-story octagonal tower built in 1890 in an older section of Tokyo, contained forty-six shops, a lounge, and three observation decks. Sadly, it was ruined in a 1923 earthquake.

It was called Ryounkaku—in English, "cloud-passer." When you think of it, that might be even better than "sky-scraper."

2

New York and Chicago

Excelsior is the state motto of New York, from the Latin meaning "higher," though it is often translated more poetically as "ever upward." Superman might suggest another alternative: "Up, up and away!" No matter how you say it, with branding like that, America's largest metropolis seems the natural location for the world's first skyscraper.

Instead, Chicago typically is accorded the honor. Its Home Insurance Building of 1885 was the first ten-story building in history to be held up primarily with an underlying metal framework, a fundamental element of all modern skyscrapers.

Yet New York City had the world's first ten-story high-rise a full decade earlier. The Western Union Building was not supported by a metal skeleton, though it did have some iron columns and beams in its masonry. Plus it was fifty feet taller than the Home Insurance Building (both were demolished long ago) and was equipped with elevators. Why doesn't it count? Or how about the first office building with passenger elevators, the eight-story Equitable Building of 1870, also in New York?

The question ultimately comes down to definitions, so those inclined to choose a side can do so with the assurance that one authoritative historian or another will have their back. Whichever city ultimately deserves the honor, both indisputably played a leading role in the story of the first skyscrapers. They continue to lead the way today, with an array of spindly, supertall towers now adding strange new shapes to both familiar skylines.

Many of New York's most impressive early commercial high-rises were the creation of George Post. Trained in civil engineering and architecture at New York University, Post supervised construction of Equitable's elevators, then got his first major solo commission with the unprecedented ten-story headquarters of Western Union. Its rooftop featured a spire with a large ball that dropped every day precisely at noon, based on a telegraph signal received from the National Observatory in Washington. The clock-setting ritual lives on to this day in the city's New Year's Eve ceremony.

Post next took on a string of Manhattan skyscraper projects, including the world's first twenty-story building for Joseph Pulitzer's *New York World* newspaper. However, he saved his biggest job for Chicago. Not only the most ambitious construction project of Post's career, but literally the largest building on the planet, the massive Manufactures and Liberal Arts Building was the grandest exhibition space of the spectacular 1893 World's Fair. With a forty-acre footprint, the structure was held up by twenty-two enormous arched iron trusses, the components for which filled six hundred railcars. (Sadly, as with nearly all of Post's New York skyscrapers, it no longer exists.)

The World's Fair was Chicago's coming out party. The booming railroad and shipping hub knitted an established East to a fertile and expanding West,

Manufactures and Liberal Arts Building, 1893 Chicago World's Fair

and it had doubled in population over the prior decade to more than a million people, passing Philadelphia to become America's second-largest city. A devastating 1871 fire had wiped out the entire central business district, but the destruction cleared the way for even more growth, drawing a stampede of ambitious young draftsmen and aspiring architects for the rebuilding effort. Their efforts led to the proliferation of a new kind of tall building that prompted the first widespread adoption of the term "sky-scraper." Yet Chicagoans still felt disrespected, and not without reason. Perhaps they had read what Rudyard Kipling wrote of their city in 1890: "Having seen it, I desire never to see it again. It is inhabited by savages."

The fair's organizers appointed Chicago's most celebrated skyscraper architect, Daniel Burnham, to oversee the crash project of planning and erecting two hundred buildings upon a square mile of lakefront parkland in just two years. Burnham recruited Post, along with four other prominent East Coast architects, and offered them full artistic freedom if each would create one of the fair's centerpiece buildings. Chicago architects took issue with his snub of homegrown firms, so Burnham brought five of them on board also to show off the city's ample supply of talent. Together, the group settled on a common motif for their monumental designs: Beaux-Arts, with rooflines at a uniform height.

Despite daunting construction setbacks, the death of his trusted design partner John Root, and the onset of a nationwide depression, Burnham miraculously had the fair ready for opening day. Twenty-seven million visitors poured into Chicago during its six-month run, marveling at the "White City," as the fairgrounds came to be called, as well as the smoky but vibrant actual city eight miles north along the lakefront, its skyscrapers faintly discernible from high atop the fair's main attraction, the original Ferris Wheel. Burnham would go on to become a superstar architect, commissioned for high-profile high-rises across the country, most famously his Flatiron Building in New York.

But the Chicago architect who is today hailed as the master of his era—to many, the "father of skyscrapers"—is not Burnham, but Louis Sullivan. Sullivan vehemently rebelled against the neoclassical style preferred by his colleagues, and insisted that new buildings needed a new look. His skyscraper designs emphasized bold vertical lines and a wholly original decorative style of elaborate tracery and organic forms. "The damage wrought by the World's Fair," he declared, "will last for half a century from its date, if not longer." But while his genius was undeniable, Sullivan was far too headstrong and combative for the investors looking for someone to build their skyscrapers, and his alcoholism only made matters worse. As a result, Sullivan won only a handful of commissions outside of Chicago, and died broke and forgotten in 1924. His funeral was paid for by a former assistant whom Sullivan had fired years before, but who had nevertheless come to admire his erstwhile employer—Frank Lloyd Wright.

The World's Fair buildings, while magnificent, were only temporary, with one exception: the Palace of Fine Arts. Now the Chicago Museum of Science and Industry, it was the venue in 1922 for the annual convention of the American Institute of Architects, which saw the launch of an international competition to create "the world's most beautiful office building." The illustrious contest became a showcase for modern influences, such as Art Deco, which would eclipse the existing order for skyscrapers.

Many entrants submitted designs showing the influence of new setback rules, which forced skyscrapers to reduce their girth bit by bit the taller they rose. Enacted first in New York in 1916, the restrictions addressed a chorus of opposition that had been building for years. Tall buildings, critics said, were fast becoming a nuisance, blotting out air and the sunlight and smothering the streets below. As early as 1896, one New York notable had announced it was his "duty as a citizen" to demand a halt to their unbridled construction:

This can be stopped now by legislation before the city is irreparably damaged. If it is not stopped, the consequence must be disastrous, and redress will be almost impossible. The results of bacteriological investigation show that the evil microbes flourish and increase in damp, dark places, but that sunlight destroys their life. Our narrow streets, when lined with tall structures, will thus become unhealthy alleys...

Who was this citizen who so publicly and vociferously opposed overcrowding Manhattan with skyscrapers? None other than George Post.

* * *

New York and Chicago are unmatched in their abundance of antique skyscrapers. Narrowing the list down to a manageable size for this book was no simple task. This chapter profiles four buildings in each city, examples that display the growth and development of American skyscrapers from their earliest days. They can be grouped in pairs, one from each city, in the following categories:

- Two early "proto-skyscrapers" built without an underlying steel frame.
- Two markedly innovative structures, both by Daniel Burnham, that demonstrated the possibilities of the office tower.
- Two whose unusual and visually appealing exterior features are surpassed by spectacularly decorated lobbies of sublime craftsmanship.
- Two late-stage antique skyscrapers that helped to bring to a close the first great era of tall buildings and laid the groundwork for what was to follow.

The stories of these buildings, as described earlier, focus primarily on the people behind their construction—the investors and business tycoons who commissioned them, and how those "founding fathers" came to prominence.

Each story is accompanied by an antique postcard from the author's collection, or in cases where no postcard could be found, by an old photograph or architectural drawing of the skyscraper from its earliest days. The year given in each illustration denotes when the building opened. Buildings are arranged chronologically in this and succeeding chapters to allow readers to observe the evolution of early skyscraper styles.

* * *

MONADNOCK BUILDING — Chicago

Louis Sullivan once said two men were responsible for the creation of the modern office building. Surprisingly, neither of them was him. One was William Hale, who made elevators. The other was Owen Aldis. As a property manager and commercial real estate agent, Aldis was responsible for creating over one million square feet of office space in Chicago, chiefly in high-rises.

A New Englander by birth, Aldis followed the family career path into the law; both his father and grandfather served on the Vermont Supreme Court. But after graduating from Yale, he went west to the post-fire boomtown of Chicago, where he was admitted to the bar in 1876. When two wealthy Bostonians, Peter and Shepherd Brooks, asked Aldis if he could manage some office property they owned in the city, the job put him in touch with a pair of young and hungry architects named Daniel Burnham and John Root.

Aldis worked with Burnham and Root on a new building for the Brooks brothers (no relation to the tailors) called the Rookery. It won praise then, and continues to today, for its brilliant interior light court and richly ornamented exterior. But one of the few people who didn't fall in love with it was Peter Brooks. The older of the two brothers was stubbornly opposed to decoration, which cost extra and collected dirt and roosting pigeons. For his next big office building, Peter Brooks was adamant: Keep it simple.

Root repeatedly drew up plans, but Aldis kept shooting them down. Then, while his partner was away on a beach holiday, Burnham produced a stark design that finally passed muster with the real estate man—a simple brown brick block. It flares slightly at the top and bottom, but other than that, the shallow rippling bays of oriel windows to break up the wind are the only elements of visual interest. Named the Monadnock after a lonely New Hampshire mountain, the building caused a buzz with its barefaced facade.

It was also a bit of a location risk, situated in a low-rent warehouse district blocks away from prime commercial real estate. But the sixteen-story Monadnock proved to be such a hit, and filled up so fast, that Peter's younger brother, Shepherd, quickly bought the adjoining narrow lot to the south to

Monadnock Building, Chicago – 1891
53 West Jackson Boulevard

double its size. By that time, Burnham was occupied with the Chicago World's Fair, and the new architects, William Holabird and Martin Roche, snuck in a few decorative elements on the southern extension. They also supported it on a steel skeleton, which opened up more leasable floorspace by eliminating the need for the six-foot-thick load-bearing brick walls that hold up the original building—to this day the world's tallest brick skyscraper.

The Monadnock became the most profitable property the Brooks brothers ever owned. Aldis went on to manage one-fifth of all the office space in the "Loop." The nickname of Chicago's central business district has its origins in the loops of underground cable that pulled grip trolleys until the final years of the nineteenth century, when Chicago's cable cars were replaced by elevated trains. A line was built on Van Buren Street in front of the Monadnock's southern face in 1897, and Aldis sued. His contention that the pollution, shadows, and clamor harmed his building's curb appeal and rentability was upheld by the state supreme court, setting the precedent for many more shopkeepers and property owners aggrieved by the "El."

The Monadnock monolith is a distant ancestor of innumerable less-is-more rectangles, but it remains undeniably unique. Like most buildings its age, it endured several remodelings until the 1980s, when new owners stripped the paint off the original brick and restored the interiors by consulting old photos and drawings. Stroll through it today, starting at the somewhat cavernous north entrance, and notice how sunlight filters down into the lobby through a stairwell trimmed with ornamental cast aluminum banisters—a decorative detail that survived the stinginess of one Peter Brooks.

BENNETT BUILDING — New York

The Bennett Building is the world's tallest—make that the world's only—cast iron skyscraper, a brick tower cloaked in a painted metal shell to give the appearance of expensive carved stone. Appropriately, it was built for *New York Herald* publisher James Gordon Bennett Jr., the king of the publicity stunt.

The son of the paper's founder, a Scottish immigrant who had built his publication into a powerhouse with Civil War battlefield reports and a heavy dose of sensational crime coverage, Bennett grew up a privileged child with an insatiable appetite for adventure, sport, and spectacle. An avid yachtsman, he challenged two rich young friends in 1866 to a transatlantic yacht race from New York to the Isle of Wight in the middle of December. When he and his crew triumphed, it was front page news in the *Herald*. Bennett succeeded his father as editor and publisher a year later, at the age of twenty-six.

Seeking to boost circulation, he dreamed up the paper's most legendary stunt in 1871, sending reporter Henry Stanley to Africa in search of Dr. David Livingstone. The celebrated missionary and explorer had gone missing on an expedition to discover the source of the Nile, and Stanley's daring exploits and ultimate success—"Dr. Livingstone, I presume?"—helped build the *Herald* into New York's biggest daily. Not every stunt had such a favorable ending. A North Pole expedition Bennett sponsored failed to reach its objective, and most of the crew perished. Yet off the coast of Siberia, three islands bear the names of Bennett and his mother and sister, Henrietta and Jeannette.

This office building was commissioned by Bennett in 1872, just a few weeks after his father died. It was purely an investment property at what then was one of Manhattan's busiest intersections; the newspaper had once been here, but had moved to another cast iron building on the Broadway end of the block. A bank occupied the main floor, above the storefronts lining the sidewalk level. A slow, primitive elevator that rose on a screw lifted passengers to the sixth floor, which was the uppermost when the building first opened. It would be three more years before the Western Union Building (now demolished)

21

Bennett Building, New York – 1892 (first six stories built in 1873)
93–99 Nassau Street

would open as the world's first ten-story skyscraper, a few blocks down on Broadway.

Growing business responsibilities did not slow Bennett's wild impulses. He founded the Westchester Polo Club, then for fun he paid one of his English polo instructors to ride a horse through the private gentleman's club in Newport, Rhode Island. When members failed to appreciate the humor of his prank, Bennett built a casino down the street, and soon was hosting the U.S. tennis championships there. He consorted with chorus girls, and spectacularly sundered a brief engagement to one Caroline May by showing up drunk at her family's house on New Year's Day and relieving himself into their fireplace.

After that incident and an inconclusive pistol duel with May's outraged brother, Bennett moved to France, where he launched the *Paris Herald*. He ran his newspaper empire from there, communicating with New York by transatlantic cable, and helping to found a competing cable company to break the telegraph monopoly based in Western Union's pioneering tower. He kept up his love of sports, sponsoring European grand prix for automobiles, hot air balloons, and airplanes. His superyacht "Lysistrata" boasted not only a sauna but a stable for a dairy cow, so that the captain could enjoy his favorite breakfast tipple, brandy milk punch.

Bennett sold his building in 1889 to real estate developer John Pettit, who ordered a full refurbishment. Four additional stories were built on top of the original property and given the same cast iron facing so that it now seems to have been built all at once. Tacking extra levels onto existing buildings was commonplace in that era, with skyscraper technology advancing so rapidly. But cast iron buildings, once stylish, were already outmoded when this job was finished. Facing bankruptcy, Pettit abruptly vanished and was never heard from again. The *Herald* moved uptown to quarters Bennett modeled after a Venetian palazzo, and though that building was long ago demolished, the name lives on as Herald Square. As for Bennett, he finally settled down and got married—at the age of seventy-three.

RELIANCE BUILDING — Chicago

With its shape, its sheen, and its swathes of gleaming glass, the Reliance Building seems like the only way it could fit in the 1890s is with the help of a time machine. That makes sense, because this very modern-looking antique was built for a nineteenth-century high-tech entrepreneur.

William Hale was a Connecticut store clerk with a high school education in 1857 when he moved with his father to Wisconsin and got a job in a paper mill. Rock River Paper eventually put the young man in charge of its store in Chicago. The business took off when the company expanded from wrapping and writing paper to heavy duty flour sacks and construction insulation. By 1870, Hale had earned enough to leave Rock River Paper and invest in an office building at the corner of State and Washington streets.

His timing couldn't have been worse. The Chicago Fire of 1871 consumed three square miles of the downtown, including his building. But Hale was undaunted. He started rebuilding within months, this time with a key improvement: an artesian well he drilled to fill a reservoir on the roof of the new five-story Hale Building. Not only did it supply water for the building and for hoses in case of another fire, it also powered the city's first office elevator by filling a large counterweight bucket until it was heavier than the passenger car it was attached to.

Hale's elevators—he also started a company to manufacture them—ran much quieter than early models driven by steam engines. Louis Sullivan called Hale one of the two men most responsible for the development of skyscrapers in Chicago, along with Owen Aldis. The business prospered in Chicago and beyond; passengers would board Hale elevators to ascend the Eiffel Tower. In 1887, he sold his stake to Otis Elevator and turned to real estate.

Years earlier he had sold the Hale Building and bought the property across the street, a four-story structure housing the First National Bank. It was the perfect spot for his own skyscraper, if he could wait out the leases. The ground floor tenant's expired in 1890, but the bank still had rights to the upper floors. So Hale brought in his friend Daniel Burnham and his partner

Reliance Building, Chicago – 1895
1 West Washington Street

John Root, who put the building on jacks. They demolished the ground floor and basement, dug a new foundation, and built a department store at ground level while the bank stayed open for business above the fray.

When First National's lease was up, it was time to do the reverse. The department store remained open while the bank on top was demolished and a skyscraper was erected its place. Fourteen stories of steel framing went up in just two weeks, a floor a day. Hale wanted to rent to doctors and dentists for private offices and exam rooms, so he demanded large windows and ample light. Burnham, working with architect Charles Atwood after the death of Root, delivered on that request, covering two-thirds of the street-facing facade with glass and cloaking the rest in a new kind of glazed terracotta that gleamed like a bathtub to underscore its clean and sanitary character. The Reliance Building, named to convey its practicality, also featured telephones and electricity throughout—and of course, four Hale elevators.

Hale died less than four years after the Reliance opened, but not without leaving behind another significant legacy with a similarly futuristic focus. His son George loved telescopes, so Hale built an observatory for the boy on the roof of their house. Years later, when George became a professor of astronomy at the University of Chicago, Hale built a research observatory for the college. Decades later, George would design the Palomar Observatory and its two-hundred-inch Hale refractor telescope.

Back at the Reliance, one evening in 1929, a pair of gangsters burst into the office in 809 and gunned down the dentist there in front of his patients. The unlucky practitioner turned out to have been under police investigation for another patient of his named Al Capone, who had ordered the infamous St. Valentine's Day Massacre two months earlier. Mobsters found dentists handy, see, on account of the narcotics they could prescribe.

Now guests can spend the night at the scene of the crime. After narrowly escaping demolition, the Reliance was renovated and converted into a boutique hotel. Historically accurate floors feature mahogany doors with the original brass knobs embossed with the building's name. The marble staircase, ironwork, and red marble walls in the attractive elevator lobby are all original too. But the Reliance's original Hale elevators are long gone.

FLATIRON BUILDING — New York

If anyone ever deserved to have a skyscraper named after him, it was George Fuller. The founder of a company that built hundreds of early office towers, Fuller basically invented the modern role of general contractor. But when he got his chance at immortality, the public refused to cooperate.

Fuller was a promising young draftsman who made partner at the Boston architectural firm of Peabody and Stearns and was put in charge of their New York office at the age of twenty-five. His specialty was mansions, but after designing a nine-story bank on Wall Street in 1880, Fuller had a new fascination. He left the firm, moved to Chicago, and started his own construction company, specializing in tall buildings. Leaving the conception and design phase to other architects, Fuller focused on getting their structures built, holding the stonemasons, ironworkers, plumbers, engineers, and other subcontractors to strict timetables he devised to keep the job moving efficiently, with deliveries of steel and other materials arriving precisely when they were needed. His firm built many of the city's first skyscrapers, including the Monadnock, as well as several large buildings for the 1893 World's Fair.

A year after the fair, Fuller's daughter married Henry Black, a former traveling salesman in the Pacific Northwest who had made enough to open two banks there. Black joined Fuller as a vice president, started hustling, and won skyscraper construction contracts in New York, St. Louis, Pittsburgh, and Baltimore. At the same time, his father-in-law began having health problems. Eventually diagnosed with "creeping paralysis"—now known as amyotrophic lateral sclerosis, or ALS—Fuller died in 1900 at the age of forty-nine.

Black succeeded him as president and aggressively grew the company through a series of mergers. He formed U.S. Realty, the first "skyscraper trust," which was vertically integrated, literally and figuratively, through its huge capital reserves to purchase and develop land and finance the construction projects it undertook. He also bought a narrow but expensive triangular parcel at the prominent intersection of Fifth and Broadway, at the center of the upscale shopping and entertainment district called the Ladies' Mile, and hired Daniel Burnham to design an office building.

Burnham was eager to create his first New York skyscraper. His design for what was to be called the Fuller Building—the company was independent of U.S. Realty and occupied the nineteenth floor—is a thin slice of wedding cake dripping with extravagant Beaux-Arts ornamentation. No intractable zealot like Louis Sullivan, Burnham always sought to balance artistic integrity with giving wealthy clients what they wanted. Nevertheless, he was dismayed when Black demanded a key alteration to the blueprints, tacking a one-story iron and glass shopfront onto the pointy end in order to squeeze out every last cent of potential rental income.

The design employs the wind-damping ridges of bay windows seen on such Burnham Chicago creations as the Monadnock and Reliance, though the Flatiron's are so slight as to be almost imperceptible. In any case, they seemed to have little effect, and the building was notorious for gusts that wreaked havoc on gentlemen's hats and ladies' skirts, and even blew occasional pedestrians off their feet. Nor did Burnham's creation enjoy universal critical acclaim: *Life* magazine called it "appalling," and the acclaimed New York sculptor William Partridge sneered that it was "a disgrace to our city, an outrage to our sense of the artistic, and a menace to life." But critics could not dissuade the public, who fell in love with the spellbinding edifice rising above Madison Square Park like the prow of an ocean liner—or, more prosaically, a clothes iron. Despite a publicity campaign that insisted on the name Fuller Building, it became the Flatiron by popular acclaim, and newspapers couldn't be persuaded otherwise.

Tenants were a mixed assortment, as pulp magazine and sheet music publishers and a female escort service rented space along with ticketing and insurance agencies and the Russian consulate, while a fancy restaurant occupied the basement level. Fuller's company went on to build dozens more skyscrapers, but in 1925 Black sold the one that was meant to bear the founder's name. For decades it was the home of Macmillan Publishers, but after they decamped in 2019, the owners undertook an extensive interior remodeling and exterior renovation.

Flatiron Building, New York – 1902
175 Fifth Avenue

Monroe Building, Chicago – 1912
104 South Michigan Avenue

MONROE BUILDING — Chicago

The rooftops of skyscrapers almost never look like the rooftops of houses, so the simple gabled crown of the Monroe Building immediately catches the eye. Nor is its chevron-shaped roofline the only feature that puts the building in a class by itself. The exquisitely tiled lobby is among the most magnificent of any antique skyscraper in America.

The Monroe was the last big project of Peter and Shepherd Brooks, two rich brothers who tapped their vast inheritance—their grandfather ran a marine insurance business—to speculate in the Chicago real estate market. Beginning with the Montauk Block, a ten-story building that opened in 1882, the brothers developed some of the city's first office towers, all from afar. They lived as patrician farmers on sprawling neighboring estates they built in their ancestral homestead of Medford, Massachusetts. Peter visited Chicago only once, which was one more time than Shepherd ever did. Nevertheless they were intimately involved in the design, construction, and management of their assets, communicating detailed instructions to their onsite agent, Owen Aldis.

Peter famously stripped all ornamentation from his Monadnock Building, but that was an anomaly for Brooks properties. His younger brother, Shepherd, who earned a degree in architecture from Harvard, saw to it that most of their buildings were lavishly appointed. For instance, the lobby of the Marquette Building, which opened a year after the Monadnock, remains lustrous today, with Tiffany glass mosaics and bronze busts of influential local Native Americans above each elevator door. To design the Monroe Building—at first called the Shepherd Brooks Building—the brothers turned to William Holabird and Martin Roche. The Chicago architects had drawn up the extension to the Monadnock, as well as the Marquette Building and the brothers' eponymous Brooks Building in 1910. Rather than pushing for maximum height, they kept the new tower at sixteen stories to complement the gothic University Club across the street. The lobby was covered floor to ceiling with handmade painted tiles from Rookwood Pottery.

That studio had been founded in 1880 by a wealthy Cincinnati woman,

Maria Longworth Nichols Storer, so that she and her friends could make ceramic vases. Her pieces won a gold medal at the 1889 Paris World's Fair, but Storer tired of the concern and gave it to her business manager, William Taylor. He incorporated and ramped up advertising and marketing, turning the picturesque factory into a tourism destination and cementing Rookwood's reputation as a key contributor to the artistic movement known as Arts and Crafts. Taylor also launched an architectural division at Rookwood to produce decorative faience tiles for, among other things, the New York subway.

Architects gravitated to the Monroe Building, especially the attic floors, which were kept well lit by side dormer windows. Holabird and Roche had offices there; so did Frank Lloyd Wright for a short time. But the father of the Prairie School of architecture—itself inspired by the Arts and Crafts movement—had no love for the building. He publicly ridiculed it and the University Club in a 1918 speech at the Chicago Art Institute. "A Chicago smokestack has more vitality as a work of art," Wright declared, "than the effete gray ghosts of a dubious past which now haunt the lakefront at the foot of Monroe Street." After that, the building was never taken seriously by architecture buffs.

Except for one. Retired Army Lt. Col. James Pritzker, a billionaire member of one of Chicago's most influential families and investor in local historic properties, bought the Monroe Building in 2005 and set out to meticulously and expensively restore it, in part to house his museum of military books and artifacts. The task included resurrecting Rookwood Pottery's architectural tile business, dormant since 1933, to replace the lobby's long-gone ornamental tiles. The Monroe Building was the first of two remarkable transformations for Pritzker. In 2013, the stalwart Republican campaign donor announced she wished to be known as Jennifer. Since then, she has become a vocal proponent of LGBT rights. Her foundation donated $1.35 million to a California institute to study transgender military service, and Pritzker later gave $2 million to the University of Victoria in Canada to establish the world's first endowed chair of transgender studies.

WOOLWORTH BUILDING — New York

Frank Woolworth was no kind of salesman. His first two bosses told him as much. So how did an awkward farm boy from far upstate New York become the head of a major multinational retail corporation? Above all, Woolworth was a master of the eye-catching display. For evidence, look no further than his namesake office building, a New York City landmark that once reigned as the tallest skyscraper in the world.

Raised on a potato farm on the eastern shores of Lake Ontario, Woolworth hated the drudgery so much he offered to work three months at a dry goods store in Watertown for free. He was laughed at for turning up on his first day in a flannel shirt with no collar or tie. Woolworth was also befuddled by the duties of a sales clerk, fumbling to find the right drawer for various merchandise and puzzling over the tickets needed to claim goods and get change from the cashier's desk. So they gave him the job of organizing the stockroom and arranging window displays. After a few years, Woolworth jumped to a rival store when its head sales clerk job opened up. He was so bad they cut his wages, and he sheepishly returned to his old job.

Then one day his boss had him put together a new gimmick: a table spread with pens, crocheting needles, harmonicas, soap, and other cheap goods, with a sign announcing that everything there cost a nickel. It was a success, so much so that Woolworth talked the boss into floating him $300 in inventory to open his own five-cent store eighty miles away in Utica. It made a profit, but just barely, so Woolworth repaid his loan, closed up shop, and tried again. His second storefront, opened in 1879 in Lancaster, Pennsylvania, was an unqualified success, offering an expanded product line of wares priced at five or ten cents. Soon Woolworth owned a small chain of five-and-dimes earning a penny of profit on every sale.

In 1890 he took the first of what was to become an annual European trip to hunt down suppliers of dolls, glass Christmas tree ornaments, and other items. Visiting Paris, he rode to the top of the new Eiffel Tower and gaped at the view.

Woolworth Building, New York – 1913
233 Broadway

Back in the States, Woolworth steadily expanded his retail empire to 286 stores by 1910, as well as several "three-and-sixpences" in the United Kingdom. He tracked each store's sales figures carefully and wrote regular newsletters for his managers, rewarding successful performance with bonuses and corporate shares. He also mandated a uniform red and gold storefront design and company logo and standardized store layouts. Finally, he kept prices low by negotiating and buying direct from manufacturers and by refusing to raise his female clerks' wages above the poverty line.

For someone who took great care in appearances, Woolworth was unsurprisingly obsessed with a skyscraper that would announce his power and influence. He also coveted heavy foot traffic, part of the formula for success for his stores. So he chose a site at the foot of the Brooklyn Bridge, on top of a major subway station and across from City Hall. It wasn't really for the company—corporate headquarters and Woolworth's private office and apartments only took up two floors. Rather, architect Cass Gilbert had it right when he described a skyscraper as "a machine that makes the land pay." Woolworth asked Gilbert to design a Gothic tower similar to the Houses of Parliament, which he admired; the architect also found inspiration in Flemish guild halls and civic buildings. In preliminary sketches it kept growing and growing, finally stopping at 792 feet above the sidewalk, making it the second-tallest man-made structure on Earth after the Eiffel Tower, which had so dazzled Woolworth on his first trip to Paris.

The massive building, trimmed in creamy terracotta with accents of blue, green, and gold paint, contained enough bricks to pave a road the entire length of Manhattan. It boasted twenty-seven acres of leasable space, enough offices for twelve thousand people. Woolworth paid for it in cash and made his money back within a year. For the opening night gala in 1913, President Woodrow Wilson flipped a switch in the White House and eighty thousand electric bulbs flashed on to illuminate what would come to be called the "Cathedral of Commerce."

Visitors still crook their necks in New York's most stunning office lobby. Their gaze rises past golden marble walls to vaulted ceilings richly decorated with murals and mosaics and supported by a charming coterie of carved grotesques that depict the men involved in the construction, including Woolworth himself counting nickels and dimes. Lucky tourists once could pay 50 cents to ride an elevator to the open-air observatory on the fifty-eighth floor. Now it is part of a private penthouse that listed for $79 million in 2019.

For most of the twentieth century, Woolworth stores were mainstays in cities and towns across America. For good and bad—it was at a segregated Woolworth lunch counter in Greensboro, North Carolina, that four Black college students began a nonviolent sit-in that energized the civil rights movement. The resulting boycotts and bad PR hurt the company, but it was bigger discount retailers like Wal-mart that proved its undoing. The last store closed in 1997, but the Woolworth Building stands.

EQUITABLE BUILDING — New York

When the gigantic Equitable Building opened in 1915, its 1.2 million square feet of leasable space made it the world's most capacious office building. Although the insurance company's founder, Henry Hyde, preferred to keep his name out of the headlines, in his business dealings he operated with a degree of audacity and hubris that puts such an elephantine skyscraper in perspective.

In 1850, the sixteen-year-old Hyde and his father were persuaded by a local schoolteacher to leave their village of Catskill and accompany him down the Hudson to New York City, where they hoped to make money in the relatively young business of life insurance. All three found employment at the Mutual Life Insurance Company of New York, the father as an agent, the son first as a clerk, then as the controller. The young man learned quickly, and in 1859 he privately approached the company president with a proposal to create a new business pursuing high-end clients. To Hyde's shock, the boss fired him on the spot.

Stung but unbowed, Hyde rented a room upstairs from Mutual's first floor Broadway office. He borrowed some furniture, put a box of cigars on the mantlepiece for customers, and hung a large sign out front above Mutual's announcing his Equitable Life Assurance Society of the United States. To bankroll the venture, he wooed investors with a guaranteed annual return of seven percent. They in turn compelled Hyde to accept the title of vice president, and named William Alexander, a popular New Jersey state senator, as the president and public face of the company.

Despite nominally playing second fiddle, Hyde drove the business. Under his aegis, Equitable became the first major insurance firm to train its agents, for which purpose Hyde instituted a novel business concept: sales conferences. He also poached the best agents of his competitors and offered prizes to those who wrote the most policies. More significantly, he devised a kind of speculative life insurance, called tontine, which promised higher deferred payouts to policyholders who paid their premiums faithfully for a full twenty-year term. The extra money came from the dividends forfeited

Equitable Building, New York – 1915
120 Broadway

by two groups: those who died (their beneficiaries received the policy's face value only, none of its surplus), and those forced to lapse or cancel when they no longer could afford their premiums (who forfeited everything). Widows and orphans and the poor were shortchanged, but tontines were immensely popular with more solvent investors poised to benefit from others' misfortunes.

The innovation brought a surge of cash into Equitable's coffers, which the company used for a variety of investments and which Hyde habitually treated as his own personal kitty. One of the biggest expenditures was an eight-story headquarters building on Broadway. Hyde persuaded his skeptical board to add passenger elevators, making Equitable the first office building in the world to feature them. To prove they were viable and that potential clients and customers would use them, the architect in charge of their installation, George Post, leased an office on the building's top floor.

When Hyde died in 1899, his son, James, was two years shy of his thirtieth birthday, when it had been agreed that the young vice president would succeed his father as the top executive at Equitable. But several of the influential millionaires on Equitable's board of directors had other ideas. They coveted control of the firm's huge investment pool, so when their president-in-waiting threw a hedonistic Versailles-themed ball in 1905, they capitalized on the negative publicity to push him out. A scandal snowballed, triggering a state investigation of the insurance business, and contentious hearings in Albany resulted in new regulations on the use of surplus funds.

Equitable also courted controversy with its plans for a bigger building. When in 1897 it first floated the idea for a forty-story headquarters, one real estate journal called it "a startling example of how open our cities are to attack from the audacious." By 1908 the proposal had metastasized to sixty-two stories, crowned with a gargantuan 150-foot flagpole which would have sufficed to overtop the Eiffel Tower had it been built.

One icy January morning in 1912, the Equitable building was gutted by a fire that killed six people and threatened the entire financial district before being brought under control. The terrifying blaze prompted the city to beef up its fire code to require automatic sprinklers and other safety measures.

Equitable sold the ruined block to gunpowder magnate Coleman Du Pont, who commissioned the business partner of the recently deceased Daniel Burnham to draw up a replacement office tower where the insurance company would become the primary tenant.

The skyscraper that rose from the ashes shot straight up from the sidewalk's edge to the roofline thirty-eight floors above. The new behemoth enraged its neighbors, who were cast into a shadow that even at noon stretched four blocks. It was the last straw for the city, which passed the nation's first setback ordinance the following year. The law required exterior walls to step inward at certain heights based on the width of the street to ensure sufficient sunshine reached the pedestrians below. Thus was codified the essential form of the Art Deco skyscrapers soon to follow.

Not satisfied with merely being Equitable's landlord, Du Pont also bought the company. In 1916 he launched an exploratory bid for the presidency. That went nowhere, but Du Pont did become a U.S. senator from Delaware, helping to build a family political dynasty. His building, once viewed as a public nuisance, has since undergone both literal and figurative rehabilitation and is now an official city landmark. Admirers tout its arcaded lobby, which stretches the full length of the building under two-story arched and coffered ceilings. This lovely amenity was enjoyed by Equitable staff for exactly one decade, until the company relocated to midtown in 1925.

Ironically, the city planning commission now has its headquarters and public hearing rooms in the Equitable Building. That means when New Yorkers want to vent their spleen at the latest skyscraper design outrage, they do so in the one that started it all.

TRIBUNE TOWER — Chicago

Sprung from an international architecture competition relentlessly promoted by the self-proclaimed "World's Greatest Newspaper," the Tribune Tower is arguably one of the most influential skyscrapers ever constructed. It reflects the aspirations of editor and publisher Robert McCormick, a towering man known as "the Colonel" who turned a second-class Second City paper into a nationwide media empire.

McCormick was the product of two powerful families. His paternal grandfather was the brother and business partner of Cyrus McCormick, who invented the grain-harvesting mechanical reaper. His maternal grandfather, Joseph Medill, helped to found the Republican party, then came to Chicago to be editor of the young *Chicago Tribune* and was elected mayor in the aftermath of the 1871 fire. McCormick's imperious mother, Kate, initially groomed his older brother to run the family paper. But when the young man suffered a nervous breakdown—and was personally diagnosed by no less an authority than Carl Jung as a non-functioning alcoholic—Medill McCormick quit, and Kate pressed "Bertie" to step in.

Teaming up with his cousin Joseph Patterson as co-editor, McCormick brought livelier coverage and popular feature sections and comic strips to the paper. He created a marketing research department to woo lucrative department stores and other top-dollar advertisers. He scouted out Canadian timber land for the *Tribune*'s own paper mill to slash newsprint costs. The editorial page touted rock-ribbed Republican principles with a heavy helping of patriotism, like when the United States entered World War I and the *Tribune* pointedly aimed an ultimatum at Chicago's upper crust: "Rich young man, the time for you to enlist is this morning." Both McCormick and Patterson joined the Army and saw action in France as artillery officers.

In 1922, outgrowing its offices, the *Tribune* announced a $100,000 competition to design the world's most beautiful skyscraper. More than 260 entries poured in from architects in twenty-three countries, and the newspaper publicized their drawings in its pages, in a major touring exhibition, and in a handsome souvenir bound volume. The eventual winner was a Gothic design by New York architects John Howells and Raymond Hood inspired by Rouen Cathedral. Though elegant, it was seen by some as disappointingly retrograde. Louis Sullivan called its cap with eight flying buttresses "the monster on top."

The *Tribune* contest marked the public debut of a number of novel ideas in architecture. Many thought the judges missed the obvious winner, a design by the Finnish architect Eliel Saarinen that earned second prize. The newspaper celebrated Saarinen and brought him to Chicago, where he became a professor of architecture. He never managed to build a skyscraper, though Howells and Hood cribbed his design for their next big project, the American Radiator Building in New York. His son, Eero, won fame for designing the St. Louis Arch and futuristic terminals at Dulles and JFK airports.

Tribune Tower was the second skyscraper outside the Loop, after the Wrigley Building, its Michigan Avenue neighbor on the north bank of the Chicago River. From his office on the twenty-fourth floor, McCormick would summon his editors for daily meetings and hold court with the ad agency execs who were the skyscraper's key tenants. Afterwards, he enjoyed climbing a flight of stairs to the public observatory, where he could look out over his beloved city.

Patterson eventually moved to New York to take the helm of the *Daily News*, America's first tabloid, which the company founded after the war. McCormick's views grew more strident and isolationist over the decades. A rival comic strip lampooned him as "Colonel McCosmic." One of the *Tribune*'s biggest scoops came in 1941, when it revealed America's secret contingency plans for war, exposing the supposed hypocrisy of FDR, whom McCormick loathed. Unfortunately for the newspaper, the Japanese bombed Pearl Harbor that weekend, and the point became moot.

McCormick remained forever proud of his service and was buried in his military uniform. The *Chicago Tribune* remained in the tower until 2018, when the building was converted into luxury apartments. Visitors can see, if they look up at the elaborate stonework above the front doors, the caricatured likenesses of McCormick and Patterson in combat on the Western Front.

Tribune Tower, Chicago – 1925
435 North Michigan Avenue

3

The Northeast

A decade before she stepped onto her pedestal in New York harbor, the Statue of Liberty made her first public appearance in Philadelphia. She was merely a disembodied hand then, gripping a torch visitors could climb to have a look around the grounds of the 1876 World's Fair.

If they went into town, they could observe workers on scaffolds raising the walls of Philadelphia City Hall. Like the Statue of Liberty, it was still in an early, unfinished state, but the grandiose municipal pile in French Empire trappings promised to be an awe-inspiring sight one day. Its planners proudly boasted that, when the enormous central bell tower was erected and crowned with a thirty-seven-foot bronze statue of William Penn, this would be the world's tallest building.

The city already could boast the tallest office, a proto-skyscraper called the Jayne Building. At eight stories plus an additional two-story ornamental tower, the patent medicine company headquarters achieved an altitude both unprecedented and impractical. Employees weary from climbing its stairs no doubt came to regret that their building opened in 1851, predating the dawn of passenger elevators. Nevertheless, the Jayne Building's pronounced vertical silhouette no doubt impressed the young Louis Sullivan, who worked for five months as an apprentice at an architectural firm across the street before moving to Chicago. (The building was demolished to make way for Independence National Historical Park.)

Philadelphia's Jayne Building was an unprecedented eight stories in an age before elevators. Louis Sullivan apprenticed at an architectural firm nearby.

Plagued by almost comical cost overruns and attendant delays, Philadelphia City Hall took nearly three decades to complete and was eclipsed by loftier structures long before its final brick was mortared. As Philadelphia was celebrating the centennial of the Declaration of Independence in 1876, construction resumed in the District of Columbia on its long-delayed Washington Monument. The 555-foot obelisk was finished the following decade, its pointed aluminum tip seven feet farther from the ground than William Penn's hat eventually would be. Visitors to the capital's new marvel rode to the top in a steam-powered elevator. The trip took ten minutes but the view was worth it. For a brief few years until the Eiffel Tower opened, this was as high as a person could ascend in a man-made structure anywhere on Earth.

It was actually the second Washington Monument. The first was a colossal column in Baltimore that opened in 1829, complete with an observation deck that visitors could reach via stairs. Soon after its debut, Boston erected the taller Bunker Hill Monument, an obelisk with stairs and small windows at the top, much like the one that would eventually rise in the capital.

Even before skyscrapers, American cities vied for primacy with soaring feats of engineering and architecture. But regardless of any towers they raised, the cities of the Northeast were destined to trail behind New York because of something more elemental: water.

With the opening of the Erie Canal in 1825, New York became the first port with a direct shipping route to the rapidly growing Midwest. Moving freight by water instead of wagon slashed transportation costs, handing the city an advantage in trade and commerce it would never relinquish. Rival ports desperately raced to counter its supremacy with their own expensive canal systems—and later, railroads—through the Appalachian Mountains.

Meanwhile, new ports were born on interior waterways. As the easternmost settlement with navigable access to the Mississippi via the Ohio River, Pittsburgh got its start as a boatbuilding center. The keelboat Lewis and Clark sailed in 1803 to map out the Louisiana Purchase and find a route to the Pacific was made in Pittsburgh; its crew set forth on waters that would eventually become highways for barges. In Buffalo, packed schooners sailing from Lake Michigan transferred their cargo to smaller boats for transport down the Erie Canal. The settlement grew into the world's largest grain port, with steam-powered grain elevators towering over the harbor.

Buffalo also became the first city lit by hydroelectric power, generated in turbines that harnessed the torrent feeding Niagara Falls. That was in 1896, an exciting year for Buffalonians. Their former mayor, Grover Cleveland, was in the White House. The downtown skyline had two brand new additions by famous architects from the recent Chicago World's Fair: Daniel Burnham's imposing Ellicott Square Building and Sullivan's alluring Guaranty Building. Soon citizens would receive what seemed like even more good news, when Buffalo was chosen as the site for the 1901 World's Fair.

But instead of glory, the fair brought infamy. President Cleveland's successor, William McKinley, was shot by an assassin during his visit. Buffalo's fair took on a tragic cast, so the story is seldom told of its most imaginative contribution. "A Trip to the Moon" was the first electric indoor dark ride and the fair's most popular attraction. The fanciful spaceship Luna took thirty passengers at a time on a simulated flight over a model of the fairgrounds and Niagara Falls. Upon arrival on the lunar surface, they disembarked to wander through papier-mâché caverns, meet the local residents, and visit the palace of the Man in the Moon and his entertaining retinue of dancing moon maidens.

Four hundred thousand people bought a ticket for "A Trip to the Moon." The ride was such a sensation that enterprising businessmen bought it after the fair closed, crated it up, and shipped it from Buffalo to the other end of the state. At Coney Island, the imaginary spacecraft became the centerpiece of Luna Park. Only there, instead of Niagara Falls, riders blasted off over a model of the shining skyscrapers of Manhattan.

* * *

An illustration of the Luna spaceship from the 1901 Buffalo World's Fair ride "A Trip to the Moon." It was relocated to Coney Island afterward for Luna Park.

Ames Building, Boston – 1891
1 Court Street

AMES BUILDING — Boston

The Ames Building seems much too dignified a building to upset anyone. But when it opened in 1891 at an unprecedented height just shy of two hundred feet, topping all but a couple church steeples and dwarfing the Old State House across the street, outraged lawmakers immediately slapped a 125-foot height limit on future Boston skyscrapers. Too late to stop Frederick Ames, who used architectural ensembles like this one to erase a stain from his family's reputation.

Shovels built the Ames fortune. Blacksmith John Ames was one of the first to forge the tools in colonial Massachusetts, and his son Oliver started a shovel company in 1803 in nearby Easton, which turned out to be a well-timed enterprise. As the nation expanded westward, Ames shovels dug canals, roads, and railroad beds. The California Gold Rush cranked demand even higher. When the Civil War began, the Union Army turned to Ames to supply its soldiers with shovels for digging their entrenchments, breastworks, and latrines.

By that time, the company was run by Oliver's sons. Oakes, the elder of the two, was elected to Congress in 1862. As the war began to wind down, President Abraham Lincoln summoned the congressman to the White House and asked him to take over a stalled federal construction project: the transcontinental railroad. Oakes was happy to oblige. His brother, Oliver Jr., became president of the Union Pacific while Oakes assumed the top role in the construction company handling contracts. They invested heavily and encouraged others in their circle to do likewise, including other members of Congress. Ames supplied the shovels and other tools, and within three years the project was complete, the rails hammered together with a ceremonial golden spike on the high plains of the Utah Territory.

Then newspapers started digging into the man known as the "King of Spades." In 1872, under the headline "The King of Frauds," the *New York Sun* revealed that Oakes Ames's construction company, Credit Mobilier, was a hive of corruption and overcharging, protected by bribes and coverups that enriched shareholders while costing the public millions. Ames was formally censured by his congressional colleagues and returned in shame to Easton, where he died of a stroke less than two months later. Oliver Jr. died three years after him.

The children endeavored to clear the family name. Oliver's son, Frederick, and daughter, Helen, hired the celebrated architect H.H. Richardson to design a library in their father's memory in Easton next to the shovel works. When that was finished, they had Richardson build a huge memorial hall in the town, then a railroad station. Eventually, Union Pacific hired Richardson to create a monumental pyramid honoring the Ames brothers in Wyoming at the highest point of their transcontinental line. President Rutherford Hayes attended the dedication in 1882. Meanwhile, Oakes's son (also named Oliver) ran for office and eventually became governor, and the Massachusetts legislature passed a resolution absolving his dad.

Richardson died in 1886 before he could design this skyscraper for Frederick Ames, but it is in his characteristic style, Richardsonian Romanesque. Supported solely by its thick granite and sandstone walls and no steel frame, the Ames is one of the tallest masonry office buildings ever constructed; Chicago's Monadnock beats it by nine feet. Students who step inside the entrance vestibule—after a time as an upscale hotel, the Ames recently became a dorm for Suffolk University—can admire the original mosaic arched ceiling. It's a detail Frederick Ames did not live long to appreciate. Two years after his skyscraper opened, he died of a stroke in his steamship stateroom on his way to a shareholders meeting for Union Pacific.

THE CAIRO — Washington, D.C.

The capital of the United States is also the nation's only large city without any modern skyscrapers. This is not, as many believe, because of some supposed rule that prohibits surpassing the Capitol dome or Washington Monument. Instead it is because of one antique skyscraper, the Cairo. Its creator was the enormously successful architect and developer T. Franklin Schneider, a man who was publicly reviled in the capital for lying to a jury in a failed effort to keep his murderous brother from the hangman's noose, and later was nearly murdered himself by a greedy son-in-law.

The son of German immigrants, Schneider apprenticed with a prolific German architect in Washington, D.C., and learned not only design—Schneider's house drawings won notice in national contests—but also the business of buying land and improving it at a profit. Opening his own office in 1883, Schneider started with single-family dwellings, then rolled the proceeds into bigger projects. By decade's end he was putting up rows of handsome townhouses, such as the ones that still line both sides of the 1700 block of Q Street. Schneider's mother and siblings moved in there, sharing the block with congressmen and other influential citizens. The newly married Schneider built a fifty-room mansion on the corner of Q and 18th, and the couple held their first ball there in January 1892. Their joy was not to last.

Schneider's younger brother Howard, in trouble with the law for shooting an unarmed Black man, had become smitten that spring with a young woman named Amanda Hamlink who lived a few doors down the block. A whirlwind courtship had ensued, and within a month he had convinced Amanda to secretly become his wife by threatening to shoot himself if she didn't. (Secret marriage would permit him to take her for conjugal carriage rides in the countryside, while living alone to see other women on the side.) When their covert connubiality was discovered that fall, Howard made a token effort to move in with the Hamlink family. But he soon was drinking and carousing again, and also seducing another woman. Her enraged father kicked Howard out the week after Franklin's housewarming ball. More angry confrontations and desperate entreaties followed. Finally, on January 31, Howard shot and

The Cairo, Washington, D.C. – 1894
1615 Q Street Northwest

killed Amanda and her older brother on the sidewalk in front of their house as they were walking home from church.

Franklin Schneider heard the gunshots from his mansion. As a crowd gathered, he scrambled to fix the problem. That night he led police to a pistol that had been planted in an alley near the crime scene, hoping to convince them his brother had acted in self-defense. He made the rounds of the city's newspaper offices to try to control the story, spreading rumors that the Hamlinks had soured on Howard when they found out he wasn't rich. He bribed or leaned on witnesses to lie on the stand at the ensuing murder trial. None of it worked, and his efforts backfired. His brother was found guilty, and he himself was indicted for perjury, as editorial pages railed at his transparent effort to buy off the justice system. A last-ditch appeal to the White House for clemency was rebuffed, and Howard went to the gallows on St. Patrick's Day 1893.

Months later, Schneider departed for Chicago and the World's Fair. One of its most popular attractions, just across from the ticket line for the Ferris Wheel, was the exotic "Street in Cairo." There fairgoers could see bazaars and belly dancers, camels and fortune tellers, a reconstructed pharaoh's tomb and a Bedouin sheikh who raced Arabian horses. Schneider also marveled at Chicago's skyscrapers. He was especially impressed with the distinctive round archways employed by Louis Sullivan in his creations, including the city auditorium and the fair's Transportation Building.

On his return to Washington, Schneider blended these elements into the district's first skyscraper. He secured a building permit in February, and construction was complete before the year ended. His eclectic twelve-story apartment building has Chicago-style projecting window bays that suggest the minarets of a mosque, an elaborately-carved stone facade with trumpeting elephants at the windowsills, and an entryway arch that seems directly lifted from Sullivan. Residents could enjoy a rooftop garden and café, bowling lanes in the basement, and a sizable ballroom.

It was not universally loved. Around Dupont Circle, neighbors howled over the monstrous imposition to their residential streets. *Architectural Record* denounced the Cairo as "an absurdity and an outrage." Politicians entered the fray, enacting a 110-foot height limit (the Cairo is 165 feet tall) that later became the Height of Buildings Act of 1899. With minor modifications, the law remains in force today.

The Schneiders moved into a suite at the Cairo and rented out the mansion, which became a private school for girls before it was eventually demolished. Franklin continued to build in the district, erecting nearly two thousand houses and nineteen apartment buildings during his career. He later started a business running candy stores across the country.

In 1914, the Schneiders' nineteen-year-old daughter Florence married a young attorney who had earned his law degree at Georgetown, and they took up residence at the Cairo. Within months, the man, Thomas Forney, was conspiring to murder Schneider for his inheritance. Forney and a hired hitman snuck into Schneider's hotel room during a candy business trip to Pittsburgh and attacked him in the dark with a hammer. Schneider fought them off with his umbrella but they escaped unidentified. When police showed Schneider the hat left behind by one of the thugs, he recognized it as his son-in-law's. He invited Forney to his office, and in the presence of three police officers, pointed a pistol in the young man's face until the he confessed. "We took a snake into our home, but he was so clever he completely deceived us," Schneider later raged, in words that could equally have applied to his brother.

Over time the Cairo lost its cachet as a residential property and was turned into a hotel. After Schneider's heirs sold it in 1955, the building fell into severe disrepair and became a flophouse for drug addicts and prostitutes. It also had the only ballroom that in the 1960s was willing to host a D.C. drag group's annual Miss Universe Ball. Today, fully renovated, it is again an upscale residential property, with a lobby that retains elements of its original mosaic tile flooring, marble wainscoting, and carved ceilings.

GUARANTY BUILDING — Buffalo

The person who first conceived of it died without ever seeing it, and the architectural partnership that designed it never worked together again. But together the three men produced the most beautiful skyscraper of the nineteenth century—and arguably the most beautiful ever.

Hascal Taylor first rose to prominence in Fredonia, New York, crafting the off-road vehicles of his time—simple, stable buckboard wagons with a durable suspension he patented. The Civil War brought many orders for his company's wagons. When it ended, Taylor's rugged buggies became the all-terrain vehicle of choice for oil drillers in the rough country of northwestern Pennsylvania. Taylor tried his own luck prospecting, and when he and a partner hit a well in 1874 that gushed three thousand barrels a day, he sold his stake in the wagon company and went all in on drilling.

Oil was first used for kerosene, not gasoline. Cars would not exist for several more decades. But as a lamp fuel far cheaper than whale oil, kerosene was in high demand, and the potential for windfall profits lured speculative investors. Like most of them, Taylor ran up against a bigger competitor. John D. Rockefeller had started with a refinery in Cleveland and rapidly expanded his control to drilling rigs and derricks. As his Standard Oil snapped up wells, it pressured railroads to lower their shipping rates.

Taylor at first tried a business partnership with Rockefeller, but sued him when Standard violated the contract terms by lowballing Taylor's oil. The suit was settled out of court, and Taylor spent another decade trying to make a go of his company, Union Oil, which he based in Buffalo. Eventually he surrendered to the inevitable and sold out to the Standard Oil monopoly. Then he bought some downtown property, and in 1893 he commissioned Dankmar Adler and Louis Sullivan to design Buffalo's premier office building.

The year marked a career apex for the Chicago duo. Their flamboyant Transportation Building with its immense golden archway was eliciting admiring stares from visitors at the World's Fair, while in the city their Chicago Stock Market was rising under the scaffolding. For Taylor, the partners started with a plan similar to their Wainwright Building in St. Louis, added stories and accentuated its height with prominent vertical strips, and covered every inch of its umber terracotta surface with Sullivan's intricate filigree. His unique motif of bold geometric and delicate organic shapes extended inside to a sumptuous lobby, the designs repeated in mosaics, murals, banisters, and a hypnotic art glass skylight.

But on the verge of the unveiling, with financing arranged and press speculation bubbling, Taylor had a severe stroke. He died the following month. The contractor, Guaranty Building Company of Chicago, immediately bought the project from his estate and stuck their name on what was to have been called the Taylor Building. They didn't keep it long; within two years, Guaranty refinanced the mortgage through the building's main tenant, Prudential Life, who assumed naming rights.

The Guaranty was the last project for Adler and Sullivan, who dissolved their partnership as commissions evaporated in a nationwide recession. Sullivan stayed busy writing manifestos like "The Tall Office Building Artistically Considered," published the month the Guaranty Building opened. In it, Sullivan coined his maxim that "form ever follows function, and this is the law." He called office towers "one of the most stupendous, one of the most magnificent opportunities that the Lord of Nature in His beneficence has ever offered to the proud spirit of man." And he blasted his fellow architects as unequal to the moment, "strutting and prattling handcuffed and vainglorious in the asylum of a foreign school." An artistic genius but bereft of business sense or a dimmer switch for his ego, Sullivan lived thirty more years after the essay's publication, and in that time designed only three more skyscrapers.

The Guaranty Building has survived being sandblasted and catching fire, among other perils. When the owners sought to demolish it in 1977, Senator Daniel Moynihan helped preservationists secure federal funding to save it, saying he would rather see Mount Vernon or the White House torn down. The preservationists' lawyers, Hodgson Russ, became tenants and now own the building as their headquarters. The firm has spent millions on refurbishment and an excellent interpretive center just off the amazing lobby.

Guaranty Building, Buffalo – 1895
140 Pearl Street

LAND TITLE & TRUST BUILDINGS — Philadelphia

Perhaps no man in U.S. history enriched himself through networking more effectively than Peter Widener. Starting with all-night poker sessions in his butcher shop, Widener schmoozed his way into the city's Republican political machine, then built a corporate empire of streetcars and public utilities in Philadelphia and across America.

Widener's first experience with pork barrel politics came when he was handed a Civil War contract to supply mutton to U.S. Army troops stationed near Philadelphia. After the war, the Republicans nominated him for city treasurer. Local papers denounced Widener and the rest of his ticket as corrupt and self-serving; when he won despite their protests, he performed as predicted. Contracts ballooned for construction of the huge city hall, benefiting Widener and his cronies in the construction business.

One of those was William Elkins, a former grocer and oil refiner who acted as Widener's guarantor in office and also happened to be a key shareholder in the firm that made the bricks for city hall. Elkins and Widener became best friends and lifelong business partners, and after Widener left office in 1877, they consolidated the city's seventeen independent horse-drawn streetcar lines and began replacing them with cable cars, then electric trolleys. Acquiring a bundle of small natural gas and electric companies in the city, they combined those into larger utilities and installed streetlights powered by them. Finally, the pair bought up land along the trolley routes—parcels that Widener as treasurer had spent city funds to improve with sewer and water lines—then set about developing them into neighborhoods.

On North Broad Street, an enclave of the nouveau riche, Widener and Elkins built mansions across the street from each other. When the former's son George married the latter's daughter Eleanor, the partnership was further cemented. Applying a formula that had worked so well for them in Philadelphia, the two men and their allies gained control of streetcar networks in New York, Chicago, Pittsburgh, and more than a hundred cities across the country. They cashed in on inflated corporate shares and arranged sweetheart deals for the other companies they ran, laying electrical conduits

Land Title & Trust Building (right) and Annex, Philadelphia – 1898 and 1903
100 South Broad Street

and gas lines, supplying fuel, and selling asphalt to repave the streets torn up to modernize their transit lines.

In 1896, finally ready to settle down, Widener set sail with his wife, Josephine, on their brand new 225-foot yacht for a cruise around the world. They made it as far as Bar Harbor, Maine, where Josephine died of heart failure. Widener sold the yacht to the U.S. Navy and donated their mansion to the library. Just north of the city limits, he commissioned Lynnewood Hall, a 110-room Georgian manor, for himself, his sons and their families with his vast collection of paintings and a thoroughbred horse farm and race track on the sprawling acres surrounding it. Elkins, ever loyal, built a mansion across the road.

The partners also assembled a large parcel on Broad Street a block south of city hall and offered it to Land Title and Trust, a real estate insurance company, in exchange for a stake and a seat on the board. There they hired Daniel Burnham to design a fifteen-story office tower decorated with his trademark banks of bay windows. The Chicago architect did not build to the edge of the lot but left an open light well on one side, hinting at a further annex to come next door. When it did four years later, it was also designed by Burnham, albeit in a somewhat more grandiose Beaux-Arts style and several stories taller than the original.

During construction of the annex in 1902, an eight-ton steel girder slipped from its chains and plummeted eight stories, killing one worker and barely missing the terrified Elkins, who was half-buried in a pile of rubble. His health failed and he died a year after the incident. His longtime partner lived to erect more Philadelphia skyscrapers, including the Widener Building next to city hall, which Widener toured on his final working trip downtown before his death in 1915.

Despite their immense wealth, the Wideners were never accepted among Philadelphia's high society, who lived along the Pennsylvania Railroad's original Main Line, not some upstart streetcar route. When Eleanor was scolded by the maître d' of the blueblood Bellevue-Stratford Hotel for lighting a cigarette, George retaliated by building a Ritz-Carlton directly across Broad Street. The couple set sail for Paris to hire a hotel chef, accompanied by their son, Harry, who spent the trip hunting for rare books for his collection. On the journey home, they booked passage on a new White Star luxury liner that was part-owned by Peter Widener through his holdings in an international shipping conglomerate. Four nights into the return voyage, the Wideners hosted the captain at their table in the first-class dining room. Hours later their ship, the Titanic, struck an iceberg. The Widener men stoically helped Eleanor onto the last lifeboat and bade her farewell. Harvard's Widener Library was built in memory of Harry, who was an alumnus.

The tragedy of the Titanic did not soften the hearts of the old money families. Seventeen-year-old Fifi Widener, daughter of Peter's other son, Joseph, was left off the guest list of the 1919 Assembly Ball, Philadelphia's most prestigious social event. Pressed by her father to relent, organizers pointedly sent Fifi an invitation as an out-of-town guest; her mother, from a respected old Philadelphia family, was completely snubbed according to rules ostracizing any woman who married a man outside of polite society—in other words, Joseph. But he got the last laugh. The city's art mavens had long dreamed that the Widener family art collection, with its fourteen Rembrandts, would eventually grace the main wing of the Philadelphia Museum of Art. Instead, in 1942 he donated every last piece to the National Gallery in Washington, D.C.

FRICK BUILDING — Pittsburgh

The austere classical granite slab named for Henry Clay Frick seems to be facing off against the belfry of the Allegheny County Courthouse across the street. For that it has earned the scorn of architecture aficionados, since the courthouse is the final masterpiece of H.H. Richardson. But the Frick Building was actually intended to cast a shadow not on Richardson's jewel but on Pittsburgh's first skyscraper, one named for Frick's former partner turned nemesis, Andrew Carnegie.

The two self-made millionaires both came from Scots-Irish immigrant families. Frick's grandfather owned a large whiskey distillery in rural western Pennsylvania, and the young man set a goal of becoming a millionaire by age thirty. He achieved it with shrewd investments in the local coal mines and beehive ovens to convert the coal into coke, a refined fuel for the region's steel mills. So impressed was Carnegie by Frick's business acumen that he brought the younger man into his organization as partner and eventually chairman.

But there were bumps in the road. One of the worst came in 1892, when Carnegie Steel workers threatened to strike over wage reductions. Carnegie told Frick to stand firm, then went on vacation to his castle in Scotland. When Frick instituted a lockout, workers surrounded the Homestead Works riverside mill complex, shutting it down. Frick's next ploy was to order a covert amphibious landing by two barges of armed Pinkerton guards to forcibly reopen the plant. It turned into a bloody fiasco, and the governor eventually sent in the militia to pacify the town. An anarchist and would-be assassin burst into Frick's office, shooting and stabbing the startled executive before being tackled and arrested. Frick's wounds healed, and never troubled him nearly as much as Carnegie's piercing suggestion that things would never have gotten so far out of hand had he been around.

Their long-simmering tension finally erupted in an 1899 boardroom dispute over coke prices. Carnegie jettisoned Frick from the chairman's seat and tried to force him to sell his eleven percent stake at below market value. Enraged, Frick chased the old man down the hall of the Carnegie Building,

Frick Building, Pittsburgh – 1902 (with Carnegie Building at right)
437 Grant Street

calling him a "goddamn thief." He sued Carnegie, who eventually settled out of court. And he purchased the land next door to the Carnegie Building to demonstrate once and for all which man had the bigger skyscraper. He had already been working with Daniel Burnham on the city's railroad station—Frick was a major shareholder in the Pennsylvania Railroad—plus a bank, a pink granite cenotaph for his family plot, plans for a mansion, and some further projects, so he gave this new commission to Burnham too.

Carnegie sold his company the following year to J.P. Morgan, who reorganized it as U.S. Steel and invited Frick back to serve on the board. The Frick Building was linked by aerial walkways to its smaller neighbor, which stood in its shade for decades until it was demolished. In addition to his steel interests, Frick served on several big corporate boards, including Equitable in New York, where he helped to oust the founder's son. Carnegie's philanthropy was more substantial and more celebrated, both then and now, but Frick was not averse to giving back to society. He and his banker friend Andrew Mellon became major art collectors and established museums for the public to see their paintings. Mellon gave his to establish the National Gallery of Art, while Frick's are in his former mansion in Manhattan—which he insisted must make Carnegie's mansion further down Fifth Avenue "look like a miner's shack." The two former partners never reconciled.

This is the first of three skyscrapers Frick built in a row down Grant Street, the north-south thoroughfare from the main railroad station. Above the vast marble lobby, an opalescent window depicts a dreamy goddess of fortune balanced precariously on her wheel. Visitors must crane their necks to see it, because the ground floor today was originally the basement. A decade after the building went up, it had to extend in the opposite direction when a public works project excavated a low hill to make the surrounding streets less steep. More granite cladding went onto the excavated cellar walls, but without the large windows of the original ground floor, the base now looks like the fortress Frick once created around his mill in Homestead. More marble went up on the interior walls too, an expense the owner could easily afford.

ARROTT BUILDING — Pittsburgh

A gaudily striped Venetian palazzo of a skyscraper, the Arrott Building was created for America's bathtub king. Not that tubs were in James Arrott's plans from the outset. An Irish immigrant from County Donegal, he started a fire insurance business when he arrived in Pittsburgh in 1859. But when an iron foundry he insured burned down, Arrott and two partners bought it, rebuilt it, and renamed it Standard Manufacturing. To its existing catalog of iron kettles, pots, pans, and pipes, they added a key new product line: enameled iron bathtubs.

Homeowners went mad for the gleaming white tubs, which looked so much more sanitary than the tin tubs generally in use. The two tubs a day the foundry could produce were not nearly enough to satisfy demand, so Arrott looked to expand his manufacturing facilities. In 1899, with a factory churning out two hundred tubs a day as well as pots, pans, kettles, pumps, sinks, toilets, and a variety of other enamelware, he orchestrated a merger with his competitors, forming the conglomerate that would become American Standard. Before long it would boast in its monthly magazine and its elegant gilt-edged color catalogs that the kings of England and Italy numbered among its many satisfied customers.

Then, desiring a skyscraper for his insurance and bathtub businesses and additional offices to rent, Arrott called upon a celebrated local architect. Frederick Osterling already had designed several steel-framed office towers in Pittsburgh, including the eight-story high-rise where he worked. But the eighteen-story Arrott Building would be his first true skyscraper, and he went for a showstopper. A rank of grimacing, bellowing faces line the rooftop, perhaps meant to resemble stylized Native American chiefs on the warpath, a decorative theme not uncommon in the era. False balconies adorn the east and south facades where an imagined emperor might stand and issue proclamations.

Beyond the twenty-one decorative columns incorporated into the structure, plans also called for two ostentatious but utterly pointless freestanding granite pillars flanking the entrance and lit with lamps. The Park Building, a

Arrott Building, Pittsburgh – 1902
401 Wood Street

flashy tower that had been erected nearby by New York architect George Post, had two such columns, so Osterling figured his skyscraper should get them also. Critics objected that they would impede sidewalk traffic. When Osterling defied them, the mayor sent police to arrest the workmen and blamed the architect for inciting a riot. A compromise sank two half-columns into the entry facade instead, but even they were chopped off a couple decades later in a remodeling job. The scars remain visible, but visitors who step past them through the main entry can soak in the bathtub king's extravagant lobby of veined marble and bronze.

On October 4, 1901, a crane at the construction site broke, dropping four tons of steel beams that barely missed crushing a streetcar full of commuters. Later that same night, at his thirty-sixth birthday bash, Osterling toasted his luck, and his friends gave him a marble bust of Venus. The next year, the Arrott Building was completed.

Poor James Arrott only got to enjoy his skyscraper for a few months before dying of a stroke. His sons stayed in bathtubs, so to speak; in 1910 they were caught up in a price-fixing scandal when feds busted the "bathtub trust." By 1950 the Arrott's froufrou facade was so far out of fashion that another immigrant, an Albanian named George Speros, bought it with the profits from his downtown sandwich shop. Mostly vacant by the 1970s, the building was briefly the target of a failed proposal to convert it into apartments for the elderly.

Finally, after decades of disuse, the Arrott has been remodeled into a boutique hotel. It remains the centerpiece of an ensemble of attractive antique skyscrapers in the city's former financial district.

BELLEVUE-STRATFORD HOTEL — Philadelphia

Islands are central in the story of George Boldt. He grew up on the German resort island of Rügen. He lost everything he had on an island in the Gulf of Mexico. He made millions managing a Manhattan palatial hotel. Finally, he bought a private island, and on it built a romantic castle for his wife, only to see it fall to ruin.

Boldt immigrated as a teenager and worked as a busboy and dishwasher in New York until he had saved enough to go west. He set up a modest farm on an island in Galveston Bay, but it didn't last—a flood swept away his cabin, crops, and chicken coop. So Boldt returned to New York and become a waiter in a better restaurant. His service was so attentive that a patron offered him a job managing a resort on the Hudson River near West Point.

Next Boldt was recruited to run the dining room of the members-only Philadelphia Club in the City of Brotherly Love. The opportunity also presented him with love of a non-brotherly type—he fell for his boss's teenage daughter, Louise Kehrer, and they were married in 1877. Her flair for décor and keen understanding of what was wanted by well-to-do wives made Louise an excellent partner for George. Philadelphia Club members helped bankroll them to open the Bellevue, a boutique hotel on Broad Street. Its restaurant became the talk of the town, particularly its house specialty of terrapin with sherry. Soon the Boldts had a bigger hotel across the street, renamed the Stratford, plus a large restaurant in the city and a pair of resort hotels on the Jersey shore.

Word got around to William Waldorf Astor, scion of one of New York's wealthiest families, who was planning to open the greatest hotel the city had yet seen. He recruited Boldt to help plan it, then leased it to him to run. Louise furnished the new Waldorf Hotel on Fifth Avenue with European antiques, filled rooms with fresh-cut flowers, and added female-friendly amenities such as a high tea room where gentlemen were permitted only if escorted by a lady. George peppered the floors with attentive assistant managers answering to guests' every request and introduced the concept of room service. Exorbitant prices added to the Waldorf's allure, so much so

Bellevue–Stratford Hotel, Philadelphia – 1904
200 South Broad Street

that the hotel earned back its construction costs in its first year of operation. The next-door neighbors, also Astors, went in with Boldt to build a second hotel on their half of the block and combine the two into the Waldorf-Astoria.

Besides dishes such as Waldorf salad and veal Oscar, the restaurant also popularized Thousand Island dressing, named for a resort area along the Canadian border where the St. Lawrence River flows out of Lake Ontario. The Boldts bought a private island there in 1895, and five years later George ordered a castle to be built on it as a gift for Louise. In Philadelphia, he closed the Bellevue, tore down the Stratford, and began raising in its place the Bellevue-Stratford, an opulent French Renaissance skyscraper to outdo his other famous hyphenated hotel.

But Louise fell ill as construction was underway on both projects and died at her home in 1904. Heartbroken, George halted all work on the nearly completed castle. The Bellevue-Stratford opened later that year and set a standard for luxury lodging in Philadelphia. Its manager kept striving for unparalleled service; in 1916, Boldt ordered plans for a three-hundred-foot runway on the roof for guests to land their airplanes. Cooler heads prevailed.

The Bellevue-Stratford has outlived the original Waldorf-Astoria, which was demolished to make way for the Empire State Building. But it was a near-run thing. In 1976, a century after George Boldt first came to Philadelphia, his hotel hosted the American Legion for a three-day state convention. Within a week, 130 people were hospitalized with a mysterious illness. Traced to bacteria in the hotel's air conditioning system, the outbreak of what is now known as Legionnaire's disease killed 29 people and forced the Bellevue-Stratford to close. Demolition loomed, but instead the property was thoroughly gutted and remodeled; today only the upper floors are hotel rooms, while the rest are offices. But the exterior retains its original glory, and the marble lobby remains a sight to behold. As for the castle, it was finally rescued from the elements and is now a tourist destination. Rumors have persisted since the day George died that the ghosts of him and his wife now happily haunt its hundred-plus rooms.

B&O RAILROAD BUILDING — Baltimore

Oscar Murray kept his head in a crisis. He proved it first by guiding the Baltimore & Ohio Railroad out of receivership and navigating it back into profitability. He proved it again in 1904 when a month after he became the railroad's president, the city of Baltimore burned to the ground.

The Baltimore & Ohio, or B&O as it is known by anyone who has played Monopoly, was the first railroad in the United States to carry passengers and freight. Chartered in 1827, it is so old that its first carriages were pulled by horses—and that was only because the original plan to mount canvas sails on the cars proved unrealistic. Baltimore merchants could not afford to be patient while technology evolved. The Erie Canal had linked the Hudson River to the Great Lakes and given New York harbor a crucial advantage over all other East Coast ports: direct access to the country's fertile frontier. New York's competitive threat forced Maryland and Pennsylvania to launch their own costly canal and rail projects to get over the Appalachian Mountains to the Ohio River and the Mississippi beyond.

The B&O's "Tom Thumb," America's first steam locomotive, began hauling passenger cars on a thirteen-mile line between Baltimore and the village of Ellicott Mills in 1830. Five years later the route stretched south to Washington. Samuel Morse famously sent the first telegram from the Capitol building to a Baltimore B&O depot using wires strung next to the tracks. But the carrier was always playing catch-up with the Pennsylvania Railroad, which had an easier route to build, bigger cities to connect, and the cushion of profitable rates hauling coal, oil, and other industrial cargo that the B&O's board could only dream of.

The railroad was in financial distress in 1896 when it hired Murray as first vice president. A Connecticut native and former lawyer, Murray had switched careers midstream and found success as a traffic manager for several western railroads. His specialty was logistics: coordinating train schedules and freight and passenger contracts to keep networks optimally busy and profitable. Within ten days of his hiring, Murray and the railroad's president took the B&O into receivership and were appointed by a federal judge as its

Baltimore & Ohio Railroad Building, Baltimore – 1906
2 North Charles Street

joint receivers. Thus empowered, they worked through a reorganization plan, funded with new issues of company stocks and bonds, to expand the network and rejuvenate its rolling stock. Three years later, B&O emerged from receivership with revenues up nineteen percent, driven mainly by additional freight tonnage masterminded by Murray.

His personality was a considerable asset. Murray was genial and charis-matic, popular with employees and customers alike, and mixed well with people of every station. A bon vivant known for his immaculate apparel and fancy carriages, Murray was said to be "gentle as a woman" in private conversation. He never married, and was joined by his private secretary, Thomas Molloy, on several sightseeing trips to Alaska, California, Florida, and Maine. In 1917, when Murray was dying, the younger man kept vigil at his side for days. In the will, Molloy received the largest individual bequest, along with Murray's gold watch. It all suggests Murray may have been gay. If so, the career risk, public opprobrium, and Maryland's sodomy law (only repealed in 2020) would have been strong incentives to keep it secret.

Murray became president of the B&O on January 1, 1904. On February 7, fire destroyed more than 1,500 buildings in downtown Baltimore, including the railroad's headquarters and all its records. Murray placed his trains at the city's command to haul aid and supplies for refugees. The railroad then won an exemption from Baltimore's 175-foot height limit and began construction of a Beaux-Arts headquarters just two feet shy of two hundred. The H-shaped building is thirteen stories tall, a number Murray considered lucky: He was the railroad's thirteenth president, and 13 was the number on the door of his office suite, paneled floor to ceiling with English oak and Circassian walnut with mahogany trim and marble floors.

The building served as B&O headquarters until the railroad merged with CSX in 1987. It is now a hotel, and those who ascend its imposing marble double staircase lit by stained glass windows representing Baltimore and Ohio will find an interesting historical display on the second floor. Over the entranceway arch are two reclining male figures: Mercury, the god of commerce, and a modern Prometheus cradling a locomotive under his arm.

Emerson Tower, Baltimore – 1911
21 South Eutaw Street

EMERSON TOWER — Baltimore

A rotating fifty-foot blue steel bottle of Bromo-Seltzer wearing a crown once made this building indisputably the oddest antique skyscraper in America. Perhaps the man behind it felt he needed that big a supply of the era's leading headache and indigestion medicine, considering how much personal turmoil he endured.

Isaac Emerson's ancestors fought for North Carolina in the Revolutionary War, and his father fought for the Confederacy while his mother taught the children in the family farmhouse. She died after the war, and when his father remarried, the teenaged Emerson got into a dispute with his stepmother's family and was sent to live with his aunt and uncle. He enrolled at the University of North Carolina in Chapel Hill, and paid his bills by working as a druggist for two physicians. His relationship with Emmaline Askew, a divorcee with two young daughters, caused another family scene—divorced women were seen as immoral. So he dropped out in 1879 after his junior year and they moved to Annapolis and got married. They next relocated to Baltimore, where Emerson opened three drugstores with money his father-in-law loaned him.

There Emerson perfected and began selling a hangover cure of his own invention, a granulated mixture of the painkiller acetanilide, sodium bromide, and citric acid that fizzed in water like seltzer. Within a decade it was so popular that Emerson sold his drugstores to focus solely on producing and selling Bromo-Seltzer. Propelled by national newspaper advertising and a sales incentive for druggists of one company share for every sixty dollars of product sold, he succeeded spectacularly. The family moved into a mansion on a hill northeast of downtown Baltimore, where from a formal garden lined with sculptures they could gaze upon nearby Druid Lake.

The country boy also discovered a love for the sea. Besides boating for pleasure on his steam yacht, Emerson organized the Maryland Naval Militia, and during the Spanish-American War he was tasked with guarding the coast from Cape Hatteras to Cape May. He retired from service in 1901 at the rank of captain and embarked on the first of several sightseeing voyages. In Florence,

Emerson was enchanted by the tower of the Palazzo Vecchio, and in 1910 he ordered a replica of it to be built as part of his drug factory, topped with a giant steel replica of Bromo-Seltzer's distinctive blue glass bottle. Just thirty feet wide, the building was hardly spacious; there was only room for lavatories on every third floor. But the well-lit tower was more memorable than any billboard, with the hours on the four clocks marked out by the dozen letters that spell Bromo-Seltzer.

Ike and Emma both had hot tempers. She was sued by a police captain for defamation when she let loose a tirade after getting pulled over for speeding. He built the city's luxurious Emerson Hotel in a huff after being scolded for removing his jacket in another fancy establishment. Each of them carried on an affair while keeping up appearances in public, until a fight in 1910 led to a messy divorce that was front page news in the *New York Times*. That gave birth to a story that when Emmaline got the mansion, her spurned husband built his eight-story Emersonian Apartments flush against it to block her view of Druid Lake. But the divorce settlement expressly prohibited any construction on the property while Emmaline lived there, so the so-called "House that Spite Built" was constructed only after she sold the mansion in 1913 and moved to a bigger place with her new beau (where he shot himself the following year). Isaac married a New York woman his daughter Margaret had introduced him to, and they stayed together until his death in 1931. Margaret outdid both her parents with three divorces and four husbands—the only one she didn't divorce, Alfred Vanderbilt, went down with the Lusitania.

The seventeen-ton revolving blue bottle with its crown lasted only twenty-five years until it was discovered to be structurally unsound and had to be dismantled. But the tower, now stripped of its adjoining factory, stands as a Baltimore landmark. Guides say it has the world's largest four-dial, gravity-driven, non-chiming clock, a boast that seems too specific to challenge. The building contains artist lofts and a small museum, and the upper rooms behind the clock faces and above can be rented for social events or wedding photo shoots in the romantic spirit of Baltimore's storied lovebirds, Captain Ike and Emma Emerson.

BUFFALO GENERAL ELECTRIC BUILDING — Buffalo

Buffalo earned the title of "City of Light" because of its status as an early proving ground for electricity's legendary pioneers: Tesla, Westinghouse, and Edison. But years before those inventors competed to harness the power displayed at Niagara Falls, businessmen like Charles Huntley developed and built a market of willing consumers primed to flip the switch.

Huntley, like many in his field, started out in a different branch of the energy sector: oil drilling. A native western New Yorker, he clerked in his father's hardware store and a sewing machine factory before setting off for the Pennsylvania oilfields hoping to make a fortune. He did just that, rising from bookkeeper to agent to broker and hauling in eye-popping commissions on the barrels of crude he traded. But when a speculating spree on the New York exchanges wiped out his nest egg, Huntley looked around for a fresh start. He got one with Daniel O'Day, a former Standard Oil pipeline manager pumping his wealth into an electric company in Buffalo.

O'Day's Brush Electric Light had lit the city's first streetlamps in the summer of 1881 along a mile of Lake Erie harborfront road. Curious locals crowded into the small power generating station. Within a month it had its first fatality, when an inebriated middle-aged dockworker leaned over the three-foot safety railing and grabbed the generator with both hands. (The shocking incident inspired a local dentist to invent the electric chair; once the state adopted it, the first to die was another Buffalo man.)

Meanwhile, Brush Electric partnered with Westinghouse in 1886 for the first commercial use of indoor alternating current lighting, this time at a Buffalo dry goods store. Still the company struggled with a local competitor, so O'Day brought in Huntley, who spent six months climbing poles, repairing broken lamps, firing boilers, and learning the business. Then he went to O'Day with a complete reorganization plan and became general manager. In 1892, Brush and its competitor merged to become Buffalo General Electric.

By that time, both Westinghouse and Edison's General Electric were competing to design the first electrical turbine engines that would be spun by the flow of a river, not steam. The project's backers split the difference, using Westinghouse generators of Tesla's own design while giving General Electric the contract to install twenty-two miles of transmission lines and transformers to get the voltage from Niagara Falls to Buffalo. There it powered trolleys, grain elevators, a flour mill, manufacturing industries, and thousands of lightbulbs through Buffalo General Electric.

The resulting buzz from hydroelectricity won the "City of Light" the honor of hosting the 1901 World's Fair. Huntley was on the fair's board, which chose for its centerpiece a 391-foot Electric Tower lit with thousands of lightbulbs supplied by his company. Edison was so entranced by the tower that he shot several slow panning shots of it with a movie camera he had invented. The fair was spoiled when President McKinley was shot there by an anarchist. His assassin got the chair.

When Buffalo General Electric needed new headquarters, they chose an homage to the original Electric Tower. Though not as tall or as ornate as the original, the fourteen-story octagonal shaft offered plenty of office space for the company and other tenants, plus a product showroom and a transformer station in the basement. Employees gathered for presentations in a small auditorium near the top that remains there today. At the summit was a public observation deck with searchlights that could be seen more than fifty miles away. That November they signaled to distant farm villages the winner of the 1912 presidential election by pointing steadily south, meaning Woodrow Wilson. Steady north would have meant William Howard Taft, while east was for Theodore Roosevelt, who had taken the oath of office in Buffalo under tragic circumstances eleven years before.

Some proposed naming the dazzling white building after Huntley, by then the company's president, but he demurred. He spent twenty years in the top post, and upon his death the board named his son to succeed him. A few elements of the exterior have been lost over the years, such as a sculpture of two youths admiring an electrical dynamo. But the building's white terracotta gleams, and the lobby has been restored to correct the excesses of a 1970s remodeling and dropped ceiling. The globe on top is no longer covered in gold leaf, but there's gilding to spare in the ceiling mural of the extravagant Buffalo Savings Bank across the street.

Buffalo General Electric Building, Buffalo – 1912
535 Washington Street

Custom House, Boston – 1915
3 McKinley Square

CUSTOM HOUSE — Boston

As the country's first federally-owned skyscraper, the 496-foot tower of the Custom House proclaims the power of Uncle Sam. Because it is a government building, it was exempt from a strict 125-foot height limit that Boston enacted after construction of the Ames Building. That height limit was rescinded long ago, but the Custom House dominated the city skyline into the 1970s and remains a prominent landmark for sailors seeking shelter in Boston Harbor.

That is by design. Before the United States adopted the income tax, import tariffs and customs duties were the main source of federal revenue. This building is where they were collected on goods shipped into Boston, which in the nineteenth century was the country's second busiest harbor after New York. The original custom house was built in this location in 1847 on the edge of the city's main wharf; now, thanks to infill, the water ends a couple blocks to the east. Customs agents calculated and collected the duties owed on the bales of imported sugar, wool, and manufactured goods that stevedores offloaded from the cargo holds from the ships moored nearby.

The job of collector was a plum political appointment, one which enjoyed significant financial spoils from the collection. At the turn of the century, it was held by a lawyer named George Lyman who had been plucked by President McKinley from the chairmanship of the state Republican committee for the role. Lyman was soon calling on a new boss, Theodore Roosevelt, to complain that the building was well past its fiftieth birthday and no longer cutting it. Built for ninety clerks, the office now employed 234, many of them squeezed into the damp basement with insufficient bathrooms or ventilation and no space for filing cabinets.

After searching without success for a suitable location, and deciding the original custom house "was such a perfect specimen of architecture that it would be a shame to mar its beauty," a special government committee decided to put a skyscraper on top of the original structure, preserving its colonnaded facade and its marble interior and dome. Because the clay beneath the original structure could not bear such a gigantic load, builders plunged concrete caissons one hundred feet down to serve as a sturdy base for the steel

81

girders. And they built big: When it opened in 1915, the thirty-story tower's blueprint included twelve vacant floors to allow room for future expansion.

The designers of this granite monolith were Robert Peabody and John Stearns, founders of a renowned Boston architectural firm. The Custom House tower was certainly one of their tallest buildings, but it wasn't their first experience with a big construction site—they had also designed Machinery Hall for the 1893 Chicago World's Fair. The Custom House tower was one of their final projects together; both men died in 1917 at their summer homes within a week of each other.

With the growth of income and payroll taxes, tariffs and customs duties shrank in importance for balancing the federal budget. In 1986 the building was vacated as government workers moved to new offices. The property was converted into a timeshare hotel in 1997. Luckily, the owners have maintained the multistory lobby, including the impressive interior dome crowned with the presidential seal, awarded to the building when native son John F. Kennedy was in the Oval Office and visible through a large circular opening through the middle of the first and second floors. The rotunda is ringed with unfamiliar flags once flown by prominent merchant shipping firms of centuries ago. The space also has several interesting glass cases of ledgers and tools that customs agents used in their work, such as hydrometers to measure the proof of liquor shipped in casks to determine the appropriate tariff.

Above the clock faces, a thrilling outdoor observatory wraps around all four sides, giving unmatched views of the harbor, the Old North Church steeple, and the jets landing at Logan Airport. It is undeniably one of Boston's best tourist attractions, in part because it is never crowded. Access is open to the public, but only by advance reservation at the front desk for a nominal fee.

4

The Midwest

nyone visiting the St. Louis World's Fair of 1904 who had attended the one in Chicago eleven years earlier must have felt on familiar territory. Again they strolled beneath grand Beaux-Arts facades studded with electric lightbulbs and boarded gondolas for scenic pleasure cruises in the central lagoon. On the midway, they could revisit the popular "Street in Cairo" attraction and could even ride the original Ferris Wheel from Chicago, which had been hauled down and reassembled piece by piece.

Not all was familiar. The passing of a decade had brought new wonders. Fairgoers marveled at the first incarnations of the mobile phone, fax machine, and X-ray. For the first time, Americans saw a person fly, as Roy Knabenshue puttered a primitive dirigible in figure eights over the fairgrounds. Few in attendance could have predicted that in a mere two decades somebody would soar across the Atlantic Ocean—or that he would do so in an aircraft named after the very city they were visiting.

Officially called the Louisiana Purchase Exposition, the St. Louis World's Fair was meant to observe the centennial of the territorial acquisition that doubled the size of the United States. (Thomas Jefferson's real estate deal happened in 1803, but the expo ran a year behind schedule.) The host city, founded by a French fur trader and named after his king, had become the Gateway to the West, the jumping off point for the wagon trains carrying those who settled it. But before they could assemble at their Missouri embarkation point, pioneers typically took a steamboat up the Mississippi River from New Orleans. Riverboat tales became standard Americana, especially those penned by the Missourian known by the nom de plume of Mark Twain. In the twilight of his life in 1904, the venerable humorist sent a letter to the president of the St. Louis World's Fair, explaining that while "it has been a dear wish of mine to exhibit myself at the great fair and get a prize," he regrettably could not attend.

Fairgoers who did make the journey from parts east crossed the river over another technological marvel, the 1874 Eads Bridge. The masonry piers that held its steel structure above the current were sunk into the sandy river bottom to almost the height of a ten-story building—in a sense, the bridge stood on underground skyscrapers. To burrow down to the bedrock, laborers had dug underwater in giant caissons pumped full of compressed air. The technique, copied for the Brooklyn Bridge, was revolutionary. It was also terribly hazardous. Fifteen workers died during construction, and dozens more were seriously afflicted with a painful ailment doctors would only later come to understand as decompression sickness, or the bends.

The Eads Bridge crossed the Mississippi at St. Louis in 1874.

Among the multitudes mesmerized by the Eads Bridge project was a precocious Boston teenager named Louis Sullivan. As he tried to make up his mind which profession he preferred, engineer or architect, Sullivan devoured magazine stories about the Mississippi span. He later wrote that that he "followed every detail of the design, every measurement, every operation" until his "soul became immersed. ... Here was Romance, here again was man, the great adventurer, daring to think, daring to have faith, daring to do." A few years later, as a young architect, Sullivan visited St. Louis and observed the Eads Bridge project as it neared completion. He made several return trips to the city over the years for various projects, including the Wainwright Building, which many regard as the first true incarnation of the modern skyscraper.

That building was erected for a brewer who was the son of an immigrant, a combination frequently encountered in the turn-of-the-century Midwest. The populations of St. Louis, Milwaukee, and Cincinnati swelled with Germans, who in turn filled their cities with breweries and biergartens. Other arrivals from villages in Ireland and Italy came to farm the fertile river valleys and plains, while Scandinavians staked out plots in the hardier climes of the north.

Along the waterways of the Great Lakes, great industrial complexes arose as steel mills, refineries, and factories dotted shorelines from Duluth to Cleveland. In Minnesota, miners found deposits of iron ore perfect for steelmaking. Freighters loaded with it made the thousand-mile journey from the far western edges of Lake Superior to the eastern rail hubs on Lake Erie with only a single navigational stop at the locks of Sault Ste. Marie.

Having begun the nineteenth century as unsettled territory that required several military expeditions to expel its Native American inhabitants to make room for settlers, the Midwest by 1900 had four of the country's ten largest cities. Another measure of its importance could be seen in the White House. Ohio gave the nation eight presidents, a tally matched only by Virginia. Most of them held office between the 1880s and 1920s, the era when the first skyscrapers rose up in cities across the nation.

Automobiles on display at the 1904 St. Louis World's Fair.

The St. Louis World's Fair also marked the public debut of an invention that would become emblematic of the Midwest: the automobile. Visitors could eye scores of models arrayed in the hall of transportation. Those with the means could hire one out for a chauffeured tootle around the fairgrounds, perhaps to the track at nearby Francis Field, where they could take a seat in the grandstand and watch the sprinters compete for gold, silver, and bronze at the first Summer Olympics held in America. If only cars had radios then, they might have listened to "The Cascades," a lilting ragtime piece by Scott Joplin. The St. Louis composer was one of the twenty million people who made it to the fair, and like most of them, he was captivated by its centerpiece, a collection of lighted waterfalls and foaming fountains at the edge of its sculpted central lake.

* * *

NEW YORK LIFE BUILDING — Kansas City

The only antique skyscraper in this book with an identical twin, the New York Life Building in Kansas City was built at the same time and from the same blueprint as its sister structure in Omaha. Both were the first tall offices in their cities, part of an expansion plan that was eventually implicated in a major insurance scandal.

After the Civil War, Equitable boss Henry Hyde invented a type of life insurance policy that jolted the formerly staid business. The so-called tontine was a deferred benefit plan that was of more use as an investment vehicle than as a way to guarantee the financial security of one's survivors. Such policies were a boon for insurers, who were able to keep funds they had traditionally refunded to policyholders as yearly dividends. Agents were able to bamboozle clients with the scheme's fuzzy complexities, and ledgers were muddled enough to deter scrutiny. Equitable's competitors rushed to follow suit, including New York Life.

William Beers was a paymaster's yeoman in the navy before becoming a clerk in New York Life's accounting department. Ambitious and persuasive, he was promoted to controller, then actuary and vice president, and when the firm's elderly and enfeebled president died in 1885, Beers was named his successor. An autocrat who kept his boardroom in the dark about much of his dealings, Beers pushed through a plan to expand the company's Midwest markets by using some of its vast reserves to put ten-story office buildings in Kansas City, Omaha, St. Paul, and Minneapolis.

The first two were designed by leading New York architects McKim, Mead & White in the style of an Italian Renaissance palazzo. Because a ten-story palazzo would be only marginally less startling in nineteenth-century Kansas City than it would have been in fifteenth-century Florence, the design employed prominent horizontal lines to deemphasize its height. So prominent, in fact, that when a marble cutter named Jacob Echol was fired at the construction site for being drunk, he crept off to collect his thoughts, lay down on the eighth-floor ledge, and fell asleep. Luckily, someone spotted the inebriated laborer snoring on the eighteen-inch protrusion and snatched him back in through the window before he could toss and turn himself into oblivion.

Meanwhile back in New York, comptroller Theodore Banta presented New York Life's board with a report alleging executive mismanagement, including questionable withdrawals and huge unpaid overdrafts. The trustees, through dereliction or outright corruption, took Beers at his word that all was well and hushed up Banta's report. While they thanked the longtime company bookkeeper for his diligence and let him keep his job, he did not keep their secret. Three years later, in 1891, the *New York Times* published a story accusing Beers of covering up one agent's embezzlement of $370,000; further stories alleged New York Life was cheating policyholders by wasting their money on inflated salaries, questionable expenses, and extravagant buildings including the new regional headquarters. When New York Life tried to deflect, Banta wrote a whistleblower letter for the *Times* front page laying out his insider knowledge. He was fired, but the damage was done. After a state investigation found more questionable practices, Beers resigned. His golden parachute—a then-princely annual pension of $37,500—led to more uproar and was soon halved. Beers succumbed the following year to a heart attack at the age of seventy. "At least he did not die rich," wrote Burton Hendrick, a well-known muckraking journalist of the era, in a scathing exposé for *McClure's Magazine*.

Shortly after taking office, Beers's successor, John McCall, paid a visit to the Kansas City building to reassure local businesses and policyholders that the company's new regional headquarters were all wise investments. McCall enjoyed slightly more than a decade in the top post before his own fall from grace and resignation in a bribery investigation. Banta, who had been rehired in his old job, testified against his new boss at 1905 hearings in Albany before the same state reform commission that also ultimately tamed Equitable.

The Minnesota buildings are gone, but the Kansas City and Omaha ones still stand. Perched on each of their entryway arches are two-ton bronze eagles designed by the renowned Beaux-Arts sculptor Augustus Saint-Gaudens and carved by his brother, Louis. The insurance company moved out long ago, and Kansas City's building is now the office of the local Catholic diocese.

New York Life Building, Kansas City – 1889
20 West Ninth Street

Wainwright Building, St. Louis – 1892
111 North Seventh Street

WAINWRIGHT BUILDING — St. Louis

More than any other example from the early age of office buildings, this stocky ten-story by Louis Sullivan is heralded as the first instance of a wholly new kind of architecture. It was built for Catherine Wainwright, one of two women for whom Sullivan designed elegant structures in St. Louis.

Wainwright was the widow of the former owner of one of the city's numerous breweries. She dabbled in real estate, bought the vacant lot where this building stands, and was majority shareholder in a company formed to erect a high-rise on it. The other major investor was her son, Ellis, who had taken over the brewery from his father. Faced with competition from local giant Anheuser-Busch, Ellis Wainwright assembled a syndicate of British investors in 1889 to purchase his and seventeen other small breweries and reorganize as the St. Louis Brewing Association with him as president.

To design the office complex, Ellis Wainwright turned to Dankmar Adler and Louis Sullivan, the men responsible for Chicago's new Auditorium Building, a combined office, hotel, and theater complex on Michigan Avenue. One of their young draftsmen, Frank Lloyd Wright, would later relate how Sullivan rushed into the office one day, suddenly struck by inspiration while out for a walk. In just three minutes, Sullivan sketched the design, one that Wright would hail decades later as "the very first human expression of a tall steel office building as architecture."

It may not seem tall to us now, and it isn't even Sullivan's tallest building in St. Louis; his Union Trust Building, completed a year later, is bigger but virtually unknown. In contrast, the Wainwright Building's simple lines, right angles, and smooth vertical elements were a profound departure from office blocks of the era, including those by Adler and Sullivan. This was their first steel-framed skyscraper, and Sullivan divided it into a distinguishable base, middle, and top, with regimented terracotta panels carrying a seedpod motif up the walls to the top floor, where it completely overwhelms the ornamentation.

Wainwright was readying for the move to the St. Louis Brewing Association's planned offices on the seventh floor in 1892 when his wife, Charlotte, died unexpectedly at the age of thirty-four. He asked Sullivan to design a suitable mausoleum for her, and the architect did not disappoint. Unlike anything else in Bellefontaine Cemetery, the tomb consists of a large stone cube capped with a half sphere; it is unmarked with the family name, and trimmed simply with a floral border.

Catherine Wainwright passed away in 1900. That year, St. Louis streetcar workers went on strike. Their lawyer, Joseph Folk, drew such admiration that he shortly became the city's top prosecutor. From that post, Folk accused city political bosses of taking bribes to dole out concessions to the streetcar lines. That caught the ear of an editor at *McClure's Magazine*, who came to St. Louis to investigate. The blockbuster story filed by Lincoln Steffens also became the first chapter of his muckraking classic on corruption and graft in America, *The Shame of the Cities*. One of the men implicated was Ellis Wainwright, who had gotten out of the beer business to invest in trolley lines.

When a warrant was issued for his arrest, Wainwright went on the lam. He settled in Paris, taking a luxurious eight-room suite on the Champs-Élysées. Living off his fortune and collecting rent from his building, Wainwright settled into an easy retirement of motoring, golf, billiards, cards, and occasional travels on the continent with Adolphus Busch, his old St. Louis brewery rival. On one occasion, Wainwright punched a Portuguese nobleman who owed him money, eliciting the epithet "American barbarian" from the offended marquis. He finally returned and charges were dropped. In 1922 the elderly Wainwright legally adopted a young divorcee, Rosalind Velma Kendall, who became his daily companion; when that soured, he paid her off to not contest his will, which she did anyway when he died two years later.

Folk, the firebrand prosecutor, went on to become governor of Missouri. His successors use the Wainwright—now a state office building—as their office when they are in town, despite it bearing the surname of one of the state's legendary fugitives from justice. Time has not been kind to the interior, where some tile flooring and door handles and one patterned skylight are all that remain from the original. But from the sidewalk, the red terracotta is just as unique it always was. Look carefully to spot a visual treat: Sullivan used a subtly different design on each story.

MILWAUKEE CITY HALL — Milwaukee

When Milwaukee held a nationwide design contest for their city hall in 1891, few were surprised when the winning entry was a German Renaissance-insp ired design drawn up by a German-born architect. A quarter of Milwaukee's population were German immigrants, a bigger share than any other American city. And they brought more to America than beer and bratwursts; the newcomers also introduced radical political ideas from their fatherland. Within two decades of its opening, Milwaukee City Hall was home to a Socialist mayor.

Picking a winning design took longer than expected. The selection committee initially chose another castle-like rendering by Henry Cobb of Chicago. But a backlash ensued, fed by public indignation at playing second fiddle to their boisterous neighbor to the south on Lake Michigan's shoreline. The aldermen shifted their support to a plan by local resident Henry Koch, the architect of several public schools. Builders sank 2,500 wooden pilings into the marshy ground to support Koch's heavy stone and brick structure with its elaborate terracotta ornamentation and gabled roofline.

The enormous belfry was 353 feet tall even without counting its forty-foot flagpole, meaning that, for a moment in history, Milwaukee boasted a structure taller than anything to be found in Chicago or New York. Completed in 1895, the handsome city hall bookended the city's first skyscraper, a fantastic fairytale German-style pile two blocks south that had been built in 1891 for brewer Frederick Pabst.

When a young woodcarver and first-generation American named Emil Seidel returned home to Milwaukee after six years of studying and perfecting his craft in Berlin, he was hired to build a scale model of Pabst's brewery for the Chicago World's Fair. Seidel next found employment carving prototypes and patterns for a stove maker. The years in Germany had fortified Seidel's incipient left-wing leanings, and he became an active member of the Socialist Labor Party. In 1904 he was one of nine Socialists elected to the board of city aldermen, and in 1910 the voters made him the first Socialist mayor of a large American city. In office Seidel raised the minimum wage, formed the city's first public works department as well as a fire and police commission, instituted a city parks system, and called for public ownership of utilities and a tax on the assets of the city's wealthy residents.

Republican and Democrat party bosses were mortified. They banded together and put forward a respected doctor and health commissioner as their unity candidate in the next election to defeat Seidel, who was swiftly drafted as the vice-presidential nominee to run with Eugene V. Debs on the Socialist ticket in 1912. Four years later, Seidel's former city attorney, Daniel Hoan, became Milwaukee's second Socialist mayor. He was reelected six consecutive times, serving until 1940.

Milwaukee City Hall was designed before steel framing was universal, so its walls bear their own weight. They also support the building's most remarkable feature: seven stories of floating wrought iron walkways that hang dramatically over the tiled atrium floor. Illuminated by a large skylight, they create a dizzying scene viewed from the main lobby. But though intended for the simple task of getting from the stairs to the offices on each floor, the walkways became a convenient spot for committing suicide, especially during the Great Depression. After the macabre tally reached eight—seven jumpers plus a milkman so startled by one landing next to him that he suffered a fatal stroke—the city stretched protective netting across the void in 1935. It stayed for more than fifty years, until the walkways were restored to their full vertiginous glory.

The four clock faces high on the tower used to be controlled by an operator on the ninth floor. Occasional tours take visitors past his former quarters to the belfry's twelfth floor, in which hangs an eleven-ton bell named after Solomon Juneau, a fur trader and the city's first mayor. From there, it is possible to spy ships far out in Lake Michigan. Or in the other direction, another nineteenth-century structure from Milwaukee's heyday as the "German Athens": a former publishing house crowned with copper domes spiked like a Kaiser's helmet.

City Hall, Milwaukee – 1895
200 East Wells Street

Schofield Building, Cleveland – 1902
2000 East Ninth Street

SCHOFIELD BUILDING — Cleveland

The city of Cleveland is not spelled the way its founder, Moses Cleaveland, signed his name. That makes it an ideal location for the Schofield Building, designed by and built for the city's first important architect, Levi Scofield.

His grandfather, a carpenter, passed on his skills to his son, who put up one of Cleveland's first commercial buildings, a three-story brick block with offices and rooms for rent. Scofield also followed in his father's footsteps and studied architecture and engineering. The Civil War interrupted his plans, and the nineteen-year-old enlisted as a private in the artillery. He served for the duration and saw combat in numerous battles, reaching the rank of captain before the war's end, when he went back to architecture.

His first project was an insane asylum. Scofield also designed several schools and private homes, as well as prisons, including the Ohio penitentiary used in the film *The Shawshank Redemption*. In 1886 he offered his services gratis to design a memorial honoring the Civil War veterans of Cuyahoga County, which encompasses Cleveland. The memorial was planned for the city's central park at Public Square, but it aroused controversy for two reasons: first, because it required moving a marble statue of Commodore Oliver Hazard Perry, victor of the 1813 Battle of Lake Erie, and second, because it would block the lake view of a property on the square owned by an influential judge and businessman. City council retracted its permission to build the monument, and when Scofield persisted in trying to put up a construction fence around the site to start the work anyway, he was placed under arrest. He and his supporters went to court and lost, but they appealed until the Ohio Supreme Court ruled in their favor. The Cuyahoga County Soldiers' and Sailors' Memorial was finally dedicated in 1894.

Scofield also exhibited another of his war monuments at the Chicago World's Fair. "These Are My Jewels" showcased six Ohioans who served in crucial roles during the Civil War, including two Union generals who later were elected president: Ulysses S. Grant and James Garfield. Ohio's governor, William McKinley, led efforts to bring the monument to the grounds of the state capitol after the fair. He also asked Scofield to squeeze in one more statue: McKinley's old commanding officer, Rutherford B. Hayes, who was elected president after the war—as McKinley later would be too. (In all, Ohio had eight presidents in the White House, seven of them between 1877 and 1921.)

In 1901 Scofield broke ground on a fourteen-story brick office building on Euclid Avenue, the city's main downtown thoroughfare. It was on the site of his father's old commercial building, which had to be torn down. That was not the only obstacle. His sister tried to fight him in court, though she failed to stop the project. Scofield was arrested again when an overzealous city building inspector accused him of safety violations, charges which a judge later threw out of court. When his building was finished, he stuck with calling it Schofield for tradition's sake and emblazoned that name across the facade in large medallions. It was an apparent nod to his father, who had done the same with the previous building even after simplifying the spelling of his own name. From his office on the top floor, the architect enjoyed an unobscured view down the avenue to his war memorial.

The Schofield Building suffered more than most antique skyscrapers. Besides the inevitable interior remodeling, it was enveloped in a brown and beige shell of steel and enamel in 1969. Forty years later the disguise came back off, and now the restored red brick and terracotta exterior contains a hotel on the lower floors and apartments above.

Another improvement is underway at the memorial. Its bronze sculpture depicting a mortar crew with a Black soldier loading a shell is one of the country's earliest public war sculptures to show a racially integrated combat scene. Nevertheless, more than one hundred Black veterans who served in Ohio regiments of the U.S. Colored Troops were omitted from the nine thousand names originally etched on marble tablets inside the monument. In a formal ceremony in 2019, their names were read aloud and put on display in a large framed proclamation until they can be added in permanent fashion.

MERCHANTS NATIONAL BANK BUILDING — Indianapolis

Deferential as a well-mannered Hoosier, the Merchants National Bank Building, which was the tallest office building in Indianapolis for fifty years, is slightly shorter than both the Indiana Statehouse dome and the Soldiers and Sailors Monument that marks the city's central axis. The skyscraper's red brick exterior is almost hypnotically plain, with some five hundred identical windows on its three street-facing sides. But within that restrained facade can be found a luxurious bank lobby that is among the best preserved of any interior of its kind.

The bank was chartered in 1865 by five businessmen, and two years after opening they hired an energetic thirteen-year-old to be their messenger boy and janitor. John Frenzel's German immigrant parents ran a boardinghouse for railroad workers. When after a few years he earned a promotion to bookkeeper and teller, he persuaded the company to hire his younger brother Otto to replace him as messenger. A couple years after that, the two teenage boys opened their own travel agency in the bank, selling European immigrants steamship tickets so they could visit the old country.

The directors rewarded the Frenzels' industry, moving John up to cashier and Otto to bookkeeper and teller; baby brother Oscar became the new messenger. In 1882, when the last of the founders retired, the Frenzels bought his shares and assumed control. At twenty-eight, John was the youngest president of a national bank in the country. They set to work expanding the business, getting into home mortgages through savings and loans, and offering personal savings accounts and safety deposit boxes by launching the state's first trust company. They also won a key business account with Eli Lilly, who was building his pharmaceutical empire in Indianapolis.

While his younger brothers stayed focused on the bank and its related businesses, John plunged into additional responsibilities. He served on the city school board, started a natural gas company, was president and chairman of a trolley company, and invested in a brewery syndicate. His influence in the Democratic party led to his election in 1882 as the county treasurer. Four years later, he declined an offer from President Grover Cleveland to serve the

Treasury Department as comptroller of the currency, supervising all national banks. Like his brothers, Frenzel's ultimate loyalty remained with their bank.

In 1908 the Frenzels opened a four-story bank on Meridian Street while they waited for leases to expire on a plot they owned next door. Once that occurred, they brought in Daniel Burnham, who duplicated the new bank's stone walls to fill the rest of the block and then stacked thirteen stories on top of the ensemble, red brick up to a top floor faced in light stone. For many years, firefighters used the rooftop as an observation tower to spot blazes and dispatch trucks.

Otto spent two decades as bank president after John stepped aside to focus on being president of their Indiana Trust Company. Meanwhile the next wave of Frenzels—John Jr., Otto Jr., and Oscar Jr.—joined the family business. Otto died in 1925, and John returned as president; Oscar's death in 1929 left the eldest Frenzel as the sole survivor of the original brothers. He steered the bank through the stock market crash and the early years of the Great Depression, including a catastrophic string of bank failures in 1933 that led President Franklin D. Roosevelt to declare a four-day national bank holiday so the remaining institutions could reorganize and survive. It was all the stress John could handle. He died two months later at the age of seventy-nine.

John Jr. and Otto Jr. each took a turn at the head of the firm, as did Otto's son-in-law and eventually Otto III. Merchants was acquired by a Cleveland bank in 1992 before Otto IV got his chance as the seventh family member at the helm. By then they had moved to a new main office, though maintaining the skyscraper as a branch office. Eventually a longtime tenant, Indiana law firm Barnes & Thornburg, bought the building. They have preserved much of the awesome bank lobby, including four bronze teller windows set in deep green marble, with contrasting marble flooring and a vaulted coffered ceiling painted with gold leaf and supported by columns two stories high. Downstairs, the twenty-ton safe door shines in mint condition, though it no longer guards any treasure.

Merchants National Bank Building, Indianapolis – 1912
11 South Meridian Street

Union Central Building, Cincinnati – 1913
1 West Fourth Street

UNION CENTRAL BUILDING — Cincinnati

Once briefly the world's tallest skyscraper outside New York, this was designed by the same man who made the record-setting Woolworth Building, which opened the same year. Union Central Life Insurance traces its roots to Methodists who founded the company in Cincinnati two years after the Civil War. When they couldn't settle on "Union" or "Central," they turned to their bishop, Davis Clark, who with ecclesiastical diplomacy suggested they compromise and use both.

His son, Jesse Clark, after finishing college and taking a lengthy vacation in Florida, England, and France, returned to Cincinnati to become a clerk at Union Central. There he stayed for the next forty-eight years, rising steadily through the ranks to become controller, treasurer, and eventually president. Union Central grew to become Ohio's biggest corporation. It prospered particularly by making loans and mortgages for farms, a practice not widespread before Clark introduced it as treasurer. His religious faith was central throughout his life, and he oversaw the establishment of eighteen missions throughout the city to provide social services, education, and recreation for children and families in the slums. Clark gave generously to his church, helping to purchase a "Gospel automobile" and construct a riverside chapel in the city's Shantytown neighborhood. He also organized Union Central's clerks into a choral society.

Clark picked another Ohio native to design the office tower. Cass Gilbert was born in Zanesville, though his family moved to Minnesota when he was a boy. His first big job as an architect was the capitol in St. Paul, after which Gilbert moved to New York to try his hand at skyscrapers. He succeeded beyond his wildest dreams—and, unusually for most architects of his era, his Manhattan creations all are still standing. With his Woolworth Building on the drawing board, Gilbert was brought in to design Union Central's tower. Both were big. The Woolworth at 792 feet was the world's tallest building, and the Union Central at 495 feet was certainly no slouch. But while the Manhattan skyscraper unmistakably soars, the Cincinnati one reflects a stout, staid design that somewhat subdues its towering height.

Ionic columns and a pyramidal roof at its crown reflect a favored classical motif of the era: a king's tomb in the ancient Greek city of Halicarnassus that was counted among the Seven Wonders of the Ancient World. The king was Mausolus, and his name has survived down the ages in the word "mausoleum." The insurance company's offices were in the upper stories beneath the pyramid, along with an executive dining hall on the seventeenth floor whose elegant coffered ceiling has been preserved. New owners converting the tower to apartments have had to reverse an earlier lobby remodeling job that hid the bronze elevator banks with stainless steel partitions and concealed the ornate original ceiling with drop panels.

That story has something of a reverse precedent. In the late 1920s, Gilbert was hired to design stonework to cover the steel superstructure of the planned George Washington Bridge over the Hudson River. But public tastes were turning. Daniel French, who had sculpted the mammoth marble Abraham Lincoln for the memorial in Washington, argued that to cover up the steel suspension towers was a "lie" and an "abomination." Critics convinced the port authority to leave the bridge unsheathed. Gilbert's final creation was another faux Roman temple, the Supreme Court Building in Washington, D.C. He wrote privately that he hoped it would "cause some reaction against the silly modernist movement." Instead, it was the last of its kind in the nation's capital.

The Union Central Building appears monochromatic, especially from a distance, such as when crossing the John Roebling Bridge—whose eponymous creator went on to design the Brooklyn Bridge, another link between Cincinnati and New York. Up close, observers may spot faint fragments of the painted accents Gilbert applied to the terracotta, although most of the paint has washed off over the course of a century. Far easier to appreciate from sidewalk vantage are the deeply rounded edges of the lower floors' carved stone foundation blocks, an effect which makes the building appear to be resting upon gigantic Chiclets.

SOO LINE BUILDING — Minneapolis

As implied by its official name when it opened—the First National-Soo Line Building—two tenants initially laid claim to this office tower. But Minnesotans took to calling their first skyscraper solely by the railroad that is almost as fun to say as it is to spell. The Soo Line is a regional railroad that takes its name from the pronunciation of Sault Ste. Marie, the half-American, half-Canadian city straddling the rapids and shipping locks where Lake Superior drains into Lake Huron. For upper Midwesterners, it was the key waypoint in a railroad shortcut east through Canada that avoided Chicago's traffic snarls and high freight charges.

First National's president didn't even attend the opening of what would be Minnesota's tallest office building for a decade, but the Soo Line's Edmund Pennington was there. These were salad days for Pennington, who had just had a county named for him in the state's far north in gratitude for Soo Line running tracks there. Pennington, the son of a British immigrant furniture maker, had started as a switchman at age sixteen, beginning a long and fruitful career in railroading.

The Soo Line was founded in 1883 by William Washburn, who became its first president while also representing Minnesota in Congress. At least part of the self-satisfaction one would expect from such an achievement must have been modulated by the fact that he was the little brother in a New England political dynasty to rival the Kennedys. By the time Washburn graduated from college in 1857, three of his older brothers already were serving in Congress as members of the new Republican party, representing three different states: their ancestral home of Maine plus Illinois and Wisconsin.

The one in Wisconsin, who bore the delightful name Cadwallader, invited William to oversee a flour mill he had purchased at St. Anthony Falls on the Mississippi River, the future location of Minneapolis. Over the years, William and "Cad" expanded their milling operations along with their political aspirations. William's first foray in elective office saw him serving in the Minnesota state house, while his brother, the mill's absentee owner, tacked on a term as Wisconsin's governor after his congressional time was up.

Their flour business boomed, figuratively and literally. In 1878, fine dust from the rollers ignited in their massive mill. The explosion was heard ten miles away. Fourteen people were killed; the accident could have been far more lethal, but it occurred in the evening after most employees had gone home. That was also the year William became the fourth Washburn elected to Congress, representing a fourth state: Minnesota. He eventually got out of his brother's business, which became General Mills, and pooled his interests with another Minneapolis mill, owned by the Pillsbury family. The remains of both companies' nineteenth-century industrial complexes still stare each other down from opposing riverbanks at the falls today.

The railroad idea went back to 1873. William, as president of the Minneapolis board of trade, had invited his eldest brother, Israel, to come speak to the local business community. The former congressman and governor of Maine was by that time the federal customs collector for Maine's main port, Portland. At the Minnesota meeting, he recommended Minnesotans lay tracks north to link to Canada's planned transcontinental railroad, thereby securing a cheaper shipping route east for their wheat, flour, and timber. A decade later, William became the first president (and Charles Pillsbury the first vice-president) of the Minneapolis, Sault Ste. Marie & Atlantic Railroad to do just that.

Montreal investors associated with the Canadian Pacific Railway provided much of the financing for what would become the Soo Line, and by 1890 they were majority shareholders of the railroad, which stretched east through Wisconsin and across the upper peninsula of Michigan to Ontario, and west from Minneapolis through North Dakota to Saskatchewan. A century later, Canadian Pacific bought the line and absorbed it; the Canadian network based its U.S. headquarters in the Soo Line Building for a period. Now the U-shaped Soo building has been converted to apartments, and the Canadian railroad offices have shipped out to a boxy 1955 skyscraper on the other corner of the block. That one was erected for the successor of—wait for it—First National Bank, the long-dismissed first half of the tower's original name.

First National–Soo Line Building, Minneapolis – 1915
101 South Fifth Street

General Motors Building, Detroit – 1922
3044 West Grand Boulevard

GENERAL MOTORS BUILDING — Detroit

Contrary to popular belief, the "D" over the doorway of this gargantuan office building does not stand for Detroit. It instead honors Billy Durant, the founder of General Motors and the irrepressible motive force behind the corporation's early growth. Mostly forgotten today, Durant was a visionary, as consequential as Henry Ford in the birth of the American automobile industry. But he lost his company and almost everything else he owned.

The grandson of a Michigan governor and timber baron, Durant left high school before graduating and started working for the family lumber business in Flint. He discovered a talent for selling: first cigars, then patent medicines, then real estate and insurance. A chance encounter introduced him to a novel product line. Late to a meeting, he hitched a ride with a friend eager to show off his new two-wheeled horsedrawn buggy. Durant was so bowled over by its smooth spring suspension that he bought a train ticket the next day, traveled

120 miles to the workshop that built it, introduced himself to the owner, and bought the business.

Then he put his sales skills to work. First Durant entered the buggy in the Wisconsin State Fair, where it won a blue ribbon. Next he turned that publicity into an order for one hundred carts. He took it to Milwaukee next, then Chicago. By the time he returned to Flint with his sample, he had six hundred orders. Soon Flint was manufacturing so many carriages and buggies that arched signs over its streets proclaimed it "Vehicle City."

In 1904, Durant acquired a struggling Flint car company founded by David Buick. The new owner took a Buick to an auto show in New York and entered it in auto races to demonstrate its superiority, and Buick surpassed Ford as the country's leading automaker. Convinced he could succeed by offering customers a variety of styles and price ranges as opposed the one-size-fits-all Ford Model T, Durant created General Motors and began acquiring other car companies, including Oldsmobile, Cadillac, and Pontiac (then called Oakland). He even made an offer for Ford. But his breakneck expansion, along with some risky investments that turned sour, dried up GM's operating cash, and in 1910 the founder lost control of his company to a consortium of bankers.

This only motivated Durant to try harder. He plunged back into the car business with a Swiss auto racer and designer named Louis Chevrolet. They turned that company into another success, and in 1916 Durant regained control of General Motors. Back in the driver's seat, he stomped the gas. GM bought Fisher Body and several parts makers including Hyatt Roller Bearing, whose president, Alfred Sloan, was put in charge of the parts division. Sloan also showed Durant around a neighborhood three miles north of the city center where real estate was cheaper and easier to secure. Sloan knew it well, since Hyatt had recently built its offices there. Durant liked it so much he chose the same block for his offices. The roller bearing building literally was rolled across the street to a new location in order to make room for General Motors.

The architectural commission went to Albert Kahn, who specialized in automotive factories, including Ford's immense River Rouge works as well as Fisher Body Plant 21, whose battered, vacant concrete hulk still haunts Detroit. Kahn put his top designer, Wirt Rowland, on the job. Rowland chose a layout of four wings connected by a central axis to allow maximum window space for six thousand white collar workers. The complex also held auto showrooms, a 1,500-seat auditorium, residential suites for visiting executives, and two swimming pools. (Kahn designed the Fisher Building, an Art Deco masterpiece across the street, a few years later.)

Durant moved into his executive suite in the east wing in 1920. The western end wasn't finished until 1922. By then it was no longer called the Durant Building and Durant no longer had an office in it. His successor, Sloan, wrote in his 1963 memoir, the still-revered management gospel *My Years with General Motors*, that Durant was "a great man with a great weakness—he could create but not administer." The founder refused to delegate decisions. As a result, he clashed constantly with his senior managers. Some quit and became GM competitors. When the company's stock price went into a slump, Durant tried to reverse the slide by buying up shares out of his own pocket. The strategy failed, and in the aftermath he was forced to resign.

Within six weeks he had started yet another car company, Durant Motors. But though it showed early promise, its creator's attention wandered and it eventually folded. Durant spent his remaining fortune and energies speculating on the stock market; the 1929 crash wiped him out for good. Still he would not quit. His last venture was a bowling alley and hamburger joint in Flint, and his ambitions to expand it into a chain ended only after he was felled by a stroke.

General Motors stayed in its massive offices through the boom years and well past the bust, finally relocating to downtown Detroit in 2000. The old company headquarters is now a state office complex. Visitors can appreciate its regal marble corridors with barrel-vaulted ceilings, more royal palace or opera hall than office building. Its current name, Cadillac Place, comes not from the luxury GM make but from France—specifically, the explorer and fur trader who founded Detroit: Antoine Laumet de La Mothe, sieur de Cadillac.

BUHL BUILDING — Detroit

A last gasp of the classical antique skyscraper era, the Buhl Building combines Gothic and Romanesque elements with a cross-shaped footprint more common to churches than office towers. It also plays a role in a fascinating display of artistic vision rapidly evolving in one city over a single, explosively creative decade.

First, the history: The Buhls were one of Detroit's founding families, beginning with two brothers who came from western Pennsylvania and each took a turn being mayor. Frederick and Christian Buhl arrived in Detroit in 1833, when its population had not yet reached five thousand. They opened a business making and selling hats and furs, a trade they had learned from their German-born father. In addition to the beaver pelts that had first lured French trappers and explorers to the Great Lakes region centuries earlier, the Buhl brothers expanded their selection of merchandise to imports including sable, lynx, chinchilla, and Siberian squirrel.

The older brother, Frederick, was mayor first, in 1848. Besides growing the shop into one of the country's major shippers of furs, he got involved in local business circles and was instrumental in organizing a merchants exchange and board of trade. Frederick's oldest son was killed in the Civil War, so another son inherited the business.

Frederick's younger brother, Christian, enjoyed even more success. He retired from the fur trade after twenty years and started a hardware wholesale company. Elected mayor in 1860, Christian served his term in office, then invested in an iron mill back in western Pennsylvania. Next he added a controlling interest in a Detroit locomotive works and organized a copper and brass rolling mill in town. He also invested in commercial real estate, erecting a block of buildings including a bank downtown. In 1884, he remodeled those properties and consolidated them into the first Buhl Building. It housed the Detroit National Bank, which was handy, considering Christian was its president. Eventually his sons took over the hardware and industrial businesses. Two grandsons, Arthur and Lawrence Buhl, created the Buhl Land Company to tear down the original Buhl Building and put a new one in

Buhl Building, Detroit – 1925
535 Griswold Street

its place as Detroit's tallest skyscraper.

With his design of the impressive General Motors Building, Wirt Rowland found his services in high demand in Detroit. So he jumped ship to another architectural firm that promised him more money and creative leeway, and began work on the Buhl Building. Its lobby is a tried-and-true combination of marble walls and barrel vaults, but the exterior departs in significant ways from the familiar trappings of antique skyscrapers. A cross shape doubles the number of desirable corner offices on every floor from four to eight, boosting lease income potential. The terracotta tiles are of varying size and rough surface, giving the appearance of a stone cathedral. On the top floor, the private Savoyard Club boasted wrought iron candelabras and other Old World décor.

The exterior is richly decorated with detailed sculptures and reliefs by Italian immigrant Corrado Parducci. Close examination reveals several swastikas, uncontroversial good luck symbols until they were permanently tainted by the Nazis. Our modern eyes may also feel uncomfortable about the stylized Native American figures adorning the facade. These were intended to emphasize that the building had sprung from a New World quite different than the one that had supplied the classic architectural tropes.

Rowland built two more skyscrapers on Griswold Street before the decade was out, and they show how quickly Art Deco supplanted the classical look. Half a block north of the Buhl's entrance, the Penobscot Building is a stepped-back slab of granite and limestone, Michigan's tallest skyscraper for almost fifty years and still one of the most recognizable silhouettes in the city's skyline. Meanwhile, directly across from the Buhl is the Guardian Building, a tour de force in colors and geometric patterns. By all means, step inside—the lobby is a scarcely controlled riot for the optic nerve that seems to be the throne room for the Queen of Legos. But before entering, notice how Parducci's aboriginal figures morph at least as dramatically as the buildings do, from the buckskin-clad chieftains of the Buhl to the Penobscot's angular, cloaked protector to the 8-bit space Aztecs of the Guardian.

TERMINAL TOWER — Cleveland

The second-tallest building in Cleveland today was once the second-tallest building in the world. Even after Terminal Tower was eclipsed by New York's Art Deco skyscraper boom, the Cleveland landmark remained the tallest thing outside Manhattan for decades as well as its city's chief transit and retail hub. Yet this immense construction project was the product of two brothers so self-effacing and shy they skipped its dedication and listened to it on the radio instead.

If their names are any indication, Oris and Mantis Van Sweringen probably did not have an easy time growing up. Their mother died when they were young, and their father, whose leg was badly wounded in the Civil War, was an alcoholic who couldn't keep a steady job. As teenagers they tried to make money through various schemes, including bike rentals, housesitting, and a butter and eggs delivery service. Then they discovered real estate, and a plateau of abandoned farmland six miles from the city center that was the former homestead of a sect of religious celibates waiting for the end of days. Or as it is known today, Shaker Heights.

The last few Shakers had sold the property in 1892, and the Van Sweringens believed it could become a planned "garden city." They began acquiring options on the land, spreading the word among like-minded strivers about their up-and-coming upperclass neighborhood. The brothers built themselves a model house of the construction style they wanted, an idealized mix of New England and "olde" English cottage designs, nothing modern or Mediterranean. Only certain colors were allowed—both in paint and skin terms.

At first, the Van Sweringens coaxed a streetcar line to the edge of their development by paying the interest costs on its construction. But they coveted a more rapid means of transit to the city, one that did not stop at busy intersections like the trolleys did. In 1909 they bought some land in the original downtown center, called Public Square, and also along a streambed running towards the city where a freight railroad called the Nickel Plate had its right-of-way. They formed a small company in 1911 to explore building

Terminal Tower, Cleveland - 1928
50 Public Square

a commuter rail line from Shaker Heights into Public Square and putting a terminal there.

Then they made a seemingly unrelated but fateful decision. Letting their two unmarried older sisters have the Shaker Heights model home, the Van Sweringen brothers purchased a farm for themselves six miles east of Shaker Heights. When they asked the widow next door if she would sell them her land to expand, she referred them to her brother. He turned out to be Alfred Smith, the senior vice president of the New York Central, which controlled two major lines through Cleveland as well as the Nickel Plate. The men made a deal: The brothers would push for a freight terminal downtown that Smith wanted for his operations, and he would back their construction plans and sell them the Nickel Plate.

Acquiring the railroad was basically a leveraged buyout. The money came from other investors, who received in return preferred stock with a guaranteed annual dividend but no voting rights. The brothers controlled the common stock and therefore the company, as long as the investors got an acceptable annual rate of return. Gathering inertia, the Van Sweringens called on the Chicago firm Graham, Anderson, Probst & White, the successor firm of the recently deceased Daniel Burnham, and ordered up the Hotel Cleveland for their Public Square land. In 1919, a public referendum backed the brothers' plan to create a unified terminal for the city's main railroads and commuter trains in an underground terminal complex at Public Square, capped by what was supposed to be a fourteen-story office and shopping complex attached to the hotel.

By the time construction started in 1925, it had metastasized into a fifty-two-story behemoth second only to the Woolworth Building in height. It was the Roaring Twenties, and much was growing too fast for comprehension. The Van Sweringens' Shaker Heights land, which appraised for $240,000 in 1900, was now worth more than a hundred times that amount; their commuter line was transporting over two million riders a year. Thanks to further leveraged takeovers, their railroad network stretched across the country. Terminal Tower opened in 1928, and the underground terminal complex followed two years later. The project took so long to finish that its traditional classical appearance was already mired in the past, but with its immensity it became an instant symbol of the city's aspirational might.

Behind it all were two odd bachelors in neutral gray suits, with few friends and fewer hobbies, who almost never went out in public. Besides their offices and boardroom near the top floors, Terminal Tower had a three-story private suite further down, with formal oak-paneled dining room and a library that could double as a ballroom. The brothers used it for daily lunches with their senior managers and other important staff, but they seldom stayed in town overnight. Instead, at the end of each workday the spinster brothers preferred to visit their spinster sisters in the Shaker Heights house before continuing home to their sprawling farm, where Oris and Mantis, with a fifty-four-room mansion at their disposal, slept in the same bedroom.

In their suburban gamble, the brothers were spot on. Shaker Heights became, and remains to this day, one of the wealthiest and most coveted residential addresses not just in Ohio, but throughout the Midwest. But the Van Sweringens did not foresee how suburbs would trigger the ubiquity of automobiles, killing demand for commuter rail and a passenger terminal. Nor did they expect the Great Depression, which wiped out their railroad empire. Their health deteriorated as rapidly as their business. Mantis died in 1935 and Oris followed him less than a year later, both in their fifties.

Trains to Shaker Heights use the terminal, but mostly it was remodeled into a shopping mall in the 1990s that has had at best mixed success. The Rock and Roll Hall of Fame was planned for the complex but pulled out in favor of a site on the Lake Erie shoreline. The hotel is still operating, but a former big department store is now a casino. In 2019 the tower was converted into apartments, though residents share the towering vaulted lobby and station waiting room with the public. From the enclosed observation deck on the forty-second floor, it is possible to pick out the distant rising patch of green that is Shaker Heights.

5

The South

I f the South were going to rise again after the Civil War, it needed cities. The failed Confederacy had been wracked by battles conducted almost entirely on its own territory. Its rural economy had been crippled, its transportation network uprooted, its factories put to the torch. The wealthy plantation owners whose cotton fields yielded the region's chief export had been forced to relinquish their enslaved workforce, which the law had always treated as their personal property.

Former states were stripped of their standing, placed under martial law, and occupied by federal troops. Those soldiers were tasked with a daunting mission: enforcing a peaceful transition to a set of radically changed social arrangements. After centuries in bondage, Black people were now to be afforded the full fruits of citizenship, including the right to vote and hold public office. But the powers arrayed against them combined public denunciations and underhanded politics with a sinister campaign of terrorism and violence masquerading as a heroic defense of tradition.

At the war's onset, the Confederacy had only one city with more than fifty thousand inhabitants: New Orleans. The North had a dozen. At least the South's lone big city suffered only minor damage after being seized early in the war. The same was true for Nashville, which was conquered quickly and turned into a supply hub for Union forces.

They would soon be joined by new cities. Birmingham was founded in

1871 next to a hilly ridge where geologists found all three raw ingredients for making steel—iron ore, coal, and limestone. Planners named the town after England's industrial powerhouse. The largest city in Texas in 1880 was Galveston, but the discovery of oil in east Texas rapidly turned Houston and Dallas into metropolises. Miami had to wait for Henry Flagler. The former Standard Oil business partner of John Rockefeller stretched his railroad to Biscayne Bay in 1896 so he could build a resort hotel there.

Even extensive war damage was not permanent. The railroad junction known as Atlanta had grown into a hive of machine shops, foundries, and mills by 1864, when the invading Union army burned it to the ground. But the reconstruction of Atlanta was ultimately more successful than Reconstruction.

The burning of Atlanta under Union occupation

For a decade, for the most part, federal troops garrisoned throughout the South kept the peace and upheld civil rights for Black people codified in the Thirteenth, Fourteenth, and Fifteenth Amendments. Former slaves served in state legislatures and even the U.S. Congress. But relentless pressure to revoke those rights, coupled with violence and lynchings organized by terror groups such as the Ku Klux Klan, eventually wore away Washington's willpower. Occupying troops were recalled in 1877, and Black rights were systematically stripped, subverted by so-called Jim Crow laws enforcing racial segregation.

Atlanta's leaders realized that perpetual ill will was not good for business. They promoted their city as a phoenix rising from the ashes, a new center of a "New South" defined by industry and trade, and willing to forget former grievances. In 1895 the city welcomed one million visitors to the Cotton States and International Exposition, meant to showcase the region's resurgence. Instead of whistling Dixie, attendees could hum the fair's jaunty theme march, "King Cotton," composed by the former conductor of the U.S. Marine band, John Philip Sousa, beginning his career as civilian bandleader.

At the far corner of the expo grounds, between a train shed and Buffalo Bill's Wild West Show, was something fairgoers had never seen before. The Negro Building was the first designated space at such an event to display the achievements of Black people. Federal funding for the fair was conditional upon its being included. Designed and built by Black contractors, it housed art, sculpture, displays, tools, and other achievements from African American students, business owners, entrepreneurs, and philanthropists, and held nightly discussions and performances.

History was also made at the fair's opening day. For the first time in Southern memory, a formerly enslaved man was invited onto the dais to give a speech to the gathered throng. Booker T. Washington was an influential educator and activist who ran a school for African Americans in Tuskegee, Alabama. In his life, he had seen nineteen men of color elected to terms in Congress and another two to the U.S. Senate. But in 1895 there were none. The writing on the wall was clear, and Washington's words were balm to the mainly White audience.

"The wisest of my race understand that the agitation of questions of social equality is the extremest folly," Washington intoned, "and that progress in the enjoyment of all the privileges that will come to us must be the result of severe and constant struggle rather than artificial forcing." Imploring people of goodwill to work together where possible, he also explicitly recognized there were limits to cooperation: "In all things purely social we can be as separate as the fingers, yet one as the hand in all things essential to mutual progress."

The Negro Building at the 1895 Cotton States and International Exposition

While Washington saw pragmatic acceptance as the best course of action for the time being, his critics derided the speech the "Atlanta Compromise." Eight months after he gave it, the U.S. Supreme Court borrowed his language in issuing its landmark ruling in *Plessy v. Ferguson.* The justices ruled "separate but equal" accommodations did not violate the Constitution. With that, racial segregation was effectively entrenched, and Jim Crow became the law of the New South for another six long decades.

* * *

Hennen Building, New Orleans – 1895
800 Common Street

HENNEN BUILDING — New Orleans

The South's first skyscraper was erected in honor of Alfred Hennen, an attorney and constitutional law professor who defended New Orleans from the British in the War of 1812 and later helped to found the city's first Presbyterian church—in short, a man of letters with an impeccable reputation. But it was paid for from the proceeds of the biggest gambling and corruption scandal in Louisiana history.

The money came from John Morris, Hennen's son-in-law. A descendant of a founding American family that at one time owned large parts of New Jersey and New York, Morris enjoyed a luxurious life at the family estate in Throgs Neck. His father's filly Ruthless won the inaugural Belmont Stakes in 1867. That year, Morris was about to earn a much bigger purse. Lotteries, an old and mostly discredited form of government fundraising, were ready for a comeback in the cash-strapped postwar South. Morris wanted to start one in New Orleans. He ponied up a $40,000 annual fee in exchange for a twenty-five-year exclusive charter to run the Louisiana State Lottery, and supplemented those payments with frequent and bountiful bribes to legislators.

Two former Confederate generals oversaw the monthly drawing on a stage in New Orleans, but considering how much he raked in, Morris had little incentive to cheat. The lottery sold two million one dollar tickets each month, tempting gamblers with $1 million in prizes, including a $300,000 jackpot, and pocketing the rest. Because Louisiana had a monopoly on state lotteries, ninety percent of tickets were bought by bettors beyond its borders. When a defiant governor in Baton Rouge tried to shut the whole thing down, Morris used his influence to have the man impeached. Eventually the federal government stepped in. Congress in 1890 put the postal system off limits to the lottery, a decision upheld two years later by the U.S. Supreme Court. The following year, Louisiana voters rejected a twenty-year extension for Morris's gambling operation, and state lotteries again vanished from the United States, not to resurface until the 1960s.

The Yankee transplant in New Orleans needed some good publicity, so he asked Thomas Sully, the local architect who had designed the Morris family mansion on St. Charles Avenue, to draw up a skyscraper to be named in honor of Hennen. Morris had recently attended the Chicago World's Fair, and he borrowed heavily from the Chicago style for this steel-framed office building, which rests on fifty-foot pilings of cypress wood to keep it from sinking into the Mississippi delta soil. The top had a roof garden with panoramic views, occasional theatrical performances, and a cigar lounge "for gentlemen who desire to indulge in the fragrant weed," as one newspaper reported.

Hennen was certainly a worthy namesake, even if he hadn't been Morris's father-in-law. He came to the city in 1808, five years after President Thomas Jefferson had purchased New Orleans and eight hundred thousand additional square miles of unexplored country north of it from France. Hennen practiced law into his eighties; he turned down repeated offers to become a judge, preferring to teach at the university. He donated his personal law library in excess of ten thousand volumes to Tulane University. One of Hennen's former slaves, Jackson Murray, spoke well of his former master in his memoirs, saying Hennen used his connections to help Murray get a job as county assessor after emancipation.

Besides the lottery, Morris kept up the family pursuit of thoroughbred racing. When the track where his father's filly won the first Belmont Stakes was condemned to make way for a city reservoir, he built a racetrack in what was still Westchester County called Morris Park. It hosted the Belmont and Preakness when it opened in 1890, and its name remains as a neighborhood in what is now the Bronx.

Morris never saw the Hennen Building completed. He died of a stroke on his vast Texas horse ranch a few months before the opening. Today the former office building, known as the Maritime since the 1920s, has been converted into timeshare apartments. Its elaborate Beaux-Arts terracotta accents along the windows, cornice, and ninth-floor balconies are simply magnifique, perfectly suited for a city so French at heart.

ENGLISH-AMERICAN BUILDING — Atlanta

Like an unsanded prototype of New York's Flatiron, this smaller antecedent of the famous Manhattan landmark gawkily juts its sharp ledges and bay windows over the Atlanta sidewalk. The wedge-shaped tower looks like it should nestle into the V-shaped Candler Building a block away. It was named for the English-American Loan and Trust Company, though the building's owners were no more successful than the Fuller Company in stopping the public from using the more obvious nickname. The company's first president, under whose tenure this Flatiron's foundations were laid, was Georgia's first Republican governor. For more than a century afterward, he was also its only one.

Rufus Bullock grew up in Albion, New York, on the Erie Canal. Perhaps the waterway's connection to the bigger world beyond his hometown gained purchase in Bullock's mind; in any case he took to the telegraph, a novel technology for sending messages vast distances in an instant via electricity. Bullock's facility with the gadgets got him promoted to manager of American Telegraph's office in Philadelphia at the age of seventeen. A freight shipping company snapped up the telegraph whiz kid next, sending him to Georgia to develop their southern network. When the Civil War broke out, Bullock put his career before his anti-secessionist principles, aiding the Confederate army by supplying its troops and setting up and maintaining telegraph wires. When the war ended, Bullock was named president of a Georgia railroad line, until he was prevailed upon to run for governor as a Republican.

Empowered by a postwar state constitution enforced by occupying U.S. troops, the newly emancipated Black residents of Georgia voted in large numbers in 1868, sweeping Bullock to victory and electing thirty-three Black Republicans to the state legislature with him. But the vocal minority of once-dominant Democrats protested that African Americans had no right to elective office. Through intimidation and parliamentary chicanery, they rammed through a vote to unseat the legislators and replace them with their defeated Democratic rivals. The Black Republicans were barred from voting on their fate, and more than a few colleagues abstained from the vote or

English–American Building, Atlanta – 1897
84 Peachtree Street

outright betrayed them.

Governor Bullock strenuously protested. He and the expelled legislators went to Washington to testify before Congress, calling on the federal government to put things right. For a year, Congress debated the matter. Meanwhile, the Ku Klux Klan organized its Georgia chapter and the killing began. Congress returned the state to martial law for such outrages, and in 1870 the Black legislators were reinstated in Atlanta. They ratified the Fifteenth Amendment to protect suffrage regardless of race, creed, or color—though not yet sex—and their state was readmitted to the union.

But the racists were ascendant. Voter intimidation reduced Black turnout in subsequent elections, and in 1871, outnumbered and facing impeachment on specious charges of embezzlement and corruption, Bullock resigned and fled back to Albion. It wasn't far enough for his enemies; authorities arrested him there five years later and returned him to Atlanta to stand trial. But juries twice declined to convict him, and charges were dropped.

Then Bullock made a stunning choice: He stayed in Georgia. The former governor became an influential businessman. He owned a cotton mill and became president of the Atlanta Chamber of Commerce, then of the English-American Loan and Trust Company, in which capacity he presided over the erection of Georgia's first skyscraper. It was designed by Bradford Gilbert, who once hung a plumb line in his half-built Manhattan skyscraper during a severe gale. Gilbert was in Atlanta as the supervising architect for the 1895 Cotton States and International Exposition.

Bullock was master of ceremonies for the fair, and it was he who asked Booker T. Washington to speak at its opening. In what became known as the "Atlanta Compromise," the Black leader and Tuskegee Institute founder said it was understandable that formerly enslaved people clamored to hold elective office. But he urged Blacks to focus for the time being on educating themselves, on working and saving, to establish a firm footing in society. "It is at the bottom of life we must begin, and not at the top," Washington said. He also implored Whites to support their fellow citizens. In the applause at the speech's conclusion, Bullock rushed across the platform and enthusiastically shook Washington's hand, though critics later took the orator to task for his accommodating tone.

Mercifully, Bullock did not live to see Margaret Mitchell's 1936 smash hit novel, *Gone with the Wind*, which portrayed him in a most uncharitable light. "Things are going to get so bad under the benign rule of our good friend Rufus Bullock that Georgia is going to vomit him up," scowls Rhett Butler, who the text strongly hints has taken part in KKK atrocities. As for the Black legislators—many of whom were freedmen with their own small businesses before the war, all of whom braved threats and lynching to run for state office and fought defiantly to win back their stolen seats—Mitchell treats them with racist scorn: "These negroes sat in the legislature where they spent most of their time eating goobers and easing their unaccustomed feet into and out of new shoes. Few of them could read or write." When the movie came out three years later, it excised the book's most objectionable parts, though some sections make for uncomfortable viewing.

For those who appreciate things spelled out plainly, this building announces "offices" in bold block letters above its two main entrances. In addition to its primary feature, the eleven-story slab, painted a creamy beige, provides welcome morning shade for people sipping their coffee in an adjacent pedestrian mall. Patrons picking up their orders in the ground floor café must navigate around the building's exposed metal girders.

CANDLER BUILDING — Atlanta

Most antique skyscrapers have some marble on the inside. But Asa Candler, the man who launched Coca-Cola on a trajectory toward global domination, set the white stone standard. Not only did he cover his seventeen-story office building in glossy Georgia marble, he also had artists fashion a three-story grand staircase out of it for the main lobby, adorned with carved busts of his mother and father—and some terribly unsavory other characters.

Candler's father came to western Georgia after the discovery of gold there in 1829. The land was supposed to be sovereign Cherokee territory, but President Andrew Jackson cleared it for settlers, forcing out the Native Americans in what became known as the "Trail of Tears." The Candlers lived on a large farm with three dozen slaves and owned a store in the town of Villa Rica, where Asa learned the basics of running a business. His schooling was interrupted by the Civil War, which ended when he was fourteen. Though he first thought of being a doctor, Candler eventually settled on being a druggist, which required no formal education and held a potentially lucrative upside. After an apprenticeship, he went to Atlanta and got a job as a drugstore clerk, where he scraped together enough to open his own shop.

Federal food and drug regulations did not exist in the late nineteenth century. Druggists dispensed all manner of tinctures, elixirs, and quasi-medicinal concoctions, often mixed with carbonated water at soda fountains. One popular patent medicine was Vin Mariani, a French wine fortified with cocaine; Ulysses S. Grant used it to push through the pain of terminal throat cancer and finish his memoirs. An Atlanta druggist, John Pemberton, began making his own non-alcoholic version of Vin Mariani that included an extract of kola nut, a stimulant from Africa. He organized a business to manufacture the syrup, which he named Coca-Cola after its two marquee ingredients.

Pemberton was a morphine addict, perhaps from a saber wound he had suffered during the war. He was also dying, probably of stomach cancer. So he sold the company to other investors and Candler in 1888. Candler believed in Coca-Cola, which he said cured his migraine headaches. He bought out the others and sold his drugstore business to focus on Coke.

Candler was a masterful promoter, and built market share for his sugary soda with free samples for soda fountain operators paired with a huge ad spend and catchy campaigns to attract customers. Shipping costs stayed low, since the syrup was only one-eighth of the recipe—fizzy water was added at the place of purchase. National distribution soared even higher through bottling, though a skeptical Candler essentially gave away the bottling rights to a Tennessee partnership. Independent bottlers across the country scrambled for franchise rights, and while Coca-Cola forfeited centralized control of product distribution, the corporation avoided the significant costs of bottling and could sink that money into advertising.

And lawyers. Newly established federal regulatory agencies soon came after Coca-Cola in court. One potential problem was its cocaine content, which Candler reduced to almost nil with the help of a New Jersey chemical company that de-cocainized the Peruvian coca leaves used to flavor the drink. Another was caffeine—not so much from the kola nut extract, which was only a minute part of the formula, but from stimulant extracted from tea leaf sweepings. The lawyers prevailed, not only against the government, but in countless lawsuits Coca-Cola brought against knock-offs to protect its trademark.

In 1906 Candler showed guests around his new skyscraper, the tallest building in Atlanta. The ground floor housed a bank he had formed; he was also its president. Artisans from Europe had carved the friezes and reliefs around the outside to glorify the arts and sciences with the usual suspects such as Shakespeare and Michelangelo and a few era-specific figures like Buffalo Bill.

But the stairwell today has some decorations more distasteful than a bottle of Coke left out in the sun too long. Candler chose the following unrepentant racists to give pride of place next to his parents in the staircase:

- John Gordon, a former Confederate general and Democratic politician who, after losing to Rufus Bullock in the 1868 gubernatorial election, became the "grand dragon" of the Ku Klux Klan in Georgia.

Candler Building, Atlanta – 1906
127 Peachtree Street

- Charles Jenkins, Georgia's first postwar governor, who fought against the Fourteenth Amendment granting rights to former slaves, then withheld state money and fled Georgia rather than hold a racially integrated state constitutional convention as ordered by federal authorities.
- Alexander Stephens, another Reconstruction-era governor and former Confederate vice president, who publicly repudiated the precept that all men were created equal, proclaiming to the contrary on the eve of war that the cornerstone of the Confederacy rested upon "the great truth that the negro is not equal to the white man; that slavery—subordination to the superior race—is his natural and normal condition."

Atlanta got the first Candler Building; another stands near Times Square. Candler also built eponymous structures in Baltimore and Kansas City. Reputedly tight-fisted, he did donate $1 million to move tiny Emory College forty miles west to Atlanta, where it was rechartered as a university. The next year, in 1916, Candler accepted an invitation from the city's leading powerbrokers to run for mayor. He won easily, and handed the business reins to his son. A few years later, Candler gave his corporate stock holdings to his children. They cashed out immediately, to his great disappointment.

The Candler Building is now a luxury hotel where guests can linger on the staircase to admire the finely carved marble, if not the subject matter. Discreetly posted QR codes link to information about each person depicted. If that gets too depressing, check out the griffins, or the intricate patterns in the original tile floor, or two ornamental windows by the son of the famous Tiffany.

GRUNEWALD ANNEX — New Orleans

The historic bar in this stunningly appointed hotel, which became the Roosevelt in the 1920s, calls itself the home of two classic Crescent City cocktails, the Sazerac and the Ramos Gin Fizz. The bartender will prepare a canonical version of either (or both) for thirsty patrons, though neither drink was invented here.

The white terracotta tower was an expansion of the original Hotel Grunewald on the south side of the block. Its owner, Louis Grunewald, was a music teacher in Germany before coming to New Orleans, where he got a job as a church organist. In 1856 he opened a music shop that blossomed into a sheet music business and piano showroom. Two decades after stepping off the boat, Grunewald opened a music hall for concerts and operas. It burned down in 1892; unbowed, he built a hotel in its place.

The hotel merited expansion in 1905, so Grunewald bought a property known as the Mechanics' Institute on the north side of the block, intending to tear it down to make way for this sixteen-story annex with another four hundred guest rooms. Demolition crews went to work, and in the attic of the old hall they found a weathered pistol and the remains of a human skeleton—haunting evidence of the building's bloody past.

The former trade school had been a temporary postwar home of the Louisiana legislature. There, in 1866, a state constitutional convention gathered to extend voting rights to Louisiana's Black citizens. When two hundred Union veterans of color held a parade to salute their new social standing, a crowd of Democratic agitators, former Confederate soldiers, and police opened fire on them. Terrified marchers fled inside the hall for sanctuary, but the mob kept shooting through the windows, charged the doors, and hunted down their victims, killing as many as fifty and wounding another 150.

Outrage over the incident swept Republicans into office in national congressional elections that fall. For a time, people of color could vote and hold office in the South. Louisiana had two successive Black lieutenant governors, one of whom temporarily served as governor—the first African American to hold that post in U.S. history. By 1905, those days were a bitter memory.

The annex featured a dramatic colonnaded lobby stretching the length of the block and connecting both hotels. Its nightclub downstairs was set up as a cave, with plaster stalactites and a waterfall. Grunewald died a few years later, and his son sold the building in 1923. The new owners tore down the original hotel and built a second tower to match the annex, then renamed it all the Roosevelt in honor of the recently deceased president. They also promoted the manager of the hotel barbershop, Seymour Weiss, to assistant hotel manager and eventually general manager.

Weiss had a way with people. He became a confidante of the audacious progressive politician Huey Long, who kept a suite at the Roosevelt. Long was a firebrand few could top; when an opponent called him a liar in the hotel lobby, Long punched him in the face. The hotheaded but astute populist was elected governor in 1928, then senator. He was assassinated in Baton Rouge in 1936 before his aspirations could take him farther. At Long's deathbed, Weiss tried fruitlessly to get the senator to reveal the location of his "deduct box," a chest stuffed with contributions. It was never found, though a replica is displayed in the lobby.

Weiss later became principal owner of the Roosevelt and licensed its famous drinks. He appears in one of a series of four 1938 murals decorating the stylish bar, wearing a light-colored suit and eating a banana amid a clutch of celebrities at Mardi Gras. Things went bad shortly thereafter for the hotelier, who was convicted of tax evasion in 1940 and spent a year in prison. He was pardoned by President Harry Truman.

Among several eye-catching objets d'art arrayed throughout the lobby is a rosewood baby grand piano once owned by the composer Basile Barès. Grunewald published several Barès songs and employed him at the music store in the 1870s. A celebrated bandleader who performed in Paris and was in high demand every Carnival, Barès lived as another person's property until he reached his twenties. His master, Adolph Perier, ran a piano shop in New Orleans, where Barès learned to tune and repair the instruments, and also to play them. He was sixteen years old, and still a slave, when he published his first original song.

Grunewald Annex, New Orleans – 1907
130 Roosevelt Way

Empire Building, Birmingham – 1909
1928 First Avenue North

EMPIRE BUILDING — Birmingham

Depending on who is doing the talking, the Empire Building in Birmingham stands on the "heaviest corner in the South" or the "heaviest corner on Earth." The boast about big skyscrapers at this intersection originated in *Jemison Magazine*, a promotional publication put out by the son of Robert Jemison, the man behind this daintily painted terracotta office tower.

Something else weighs heavily on this corner: the legacy of slavery. Jemison's uncle had five hundred enslaved Black people working on his six plantations before the Civil War. The uncle, also named Robert Jemison, additionally had a working partnership with a remarkable slave who won his freedom through his own architectural brilliance and left a legacy all Alabamans can admire.

Besides his plantations, Jemison was a state legislator and the owner of several businesses including a bridge company. It was through that enterprise that he met Horace King, a man of mixed African and Catawba ancestry. While technically enslaved to a contractor named John Godwin, King had proven so adept at designing wooden covered bridges and overseeing their construction that Godwin paid him to travel to the job sites and supervise the work crews—including other slaves—on his own. Jemison hired King to build several bridges, and eventually grew to admire the man so much that he had a special law passed in 1846 emancipating King and allowing him to continue to work in Alabama. He and Godwin also arranged for King to travel to Ohio to be sworn into the Freemasons. Blacks were barred from joining the order in the South, but an existing membership could be honored. In 1850, Jemison saw to it that King was hired to help design and erect the state capitol building in Montgomery. King responded by devising its elegantly cantilevered double spiral staircase.

Jemison argued against secession, but remained loyal when overruled. He was president of the state senate in 1863, then represented Alabama in the Confederate senate. As for King, he was conscripted to help block Southern rivers to keep out Union gunboats, and his wife and children were toll collectors for a Georgia bridge until invading U.S. troops burned it down.

At one point King wrote to Jemison to ask what would happen if he refused to supply timbers for the hulls of Confederate ships. The senator's answer is not known, but might safely be assumed.

After the war, King had more business than he could handle rebuilding destroyed bridges, mills, and warehouses. He also followed Jemison into the Alabama House of Representatives, serving two terms in the capitol building he had helped to build. One of his sons designed the Negro Building for the 1895 Atlanta Exposition. After Godwin's death, King honored him with a stone obelisk proclaiming the "love and gratitude (King) felt for his lost friend and former master." Volunteers recently identified King's unmarked grave and placed a similar obelisk in his memory. His portrait now hangs on a wall in the state capitol next to his staircases.

Jemison and his family kept their huge, unfinished Tuscaloosa mansion after the war, though without slaves to tend their plantations they had to sell the land. His relationship with King did not sway the old man from his supremacist ideology. Political and social equality was impossible, he wrote to his brother, "between races so different in color, intellect, instincts, and habits." He died in 1871.

That year saw the founding of Birmingham, a mill town meant to exploit rich seams of coal, limestone, and iron ore in a nearby ridge. Robert Jemison's nephew Robert Jemison moved there with his family in 1884 and built a fortune investing in street railways and suburban developments. His son—yet another Robert Jemison—followed him into real estate, and launched the magazine that coined the "heaviest corner" formulation.

The Empire Building was erected in 1909 on the former site of a saloon that closed when, in rapid succession, the city, county, and state outlawed alcohol. Now a boutique hotel, its entrance is flanked by the original pink granite columns. An iron and marble staircase and chandeliers are also as they were on opening day. By far its best feature, however, is the rooftop bar, which allows a rare closeup view of the colorfully painted terracotta cornice. The sleeping maiden in the moon might be dreaming of Birmingham's other sculpted moon—the cast iron bare buttocks of Vulcan, who stands unabashed atop the crest of Red Mountain.

ADOLPHUS HOTEL — Dallas

This regal hotel opulently decorated in the style of Louis XIV, the Sun King, was paid for by the King of Beers. It is named after Adolphus Busch, who built Anheuser-Busch into the world's biggest brewing concern and made Budweiser into America's first popular mass market beer.

Busch came from vineyard country in Germany's Rhine River valley. The son of a well-to-do merchant, he studied English and French in college. As the fourth-youngest in a line of twenty-four children, Busch's prospects of inheritance were not promising, so in 1857 he followed two older brothers to America to seek his fortune. Like them he chose St. Louis, whose German immigrant population supported dozens of breweries, many specializing in the crisp lagers and pilsners favored by central European palates. Though he preferred wine to beer, this was familiar territory for Busch, who had apprenticed in an uncle's brewery back home. He set up a business to supply breweries with hops, malt, barley, and other essentials.

One of his customers was Eberhard Anheuser, a soap manufacturer who had recently acquired an underperforming brewery. Busch took a shine to Anheuser's daughter Lilly, while his older brother Ulrich did likewise with her sister Anna; the family intertwining was made official in an 1861 double wedding. Father- and son-in-law next served a mostly uneventful three-month stint together in the Union Army guarding Missouri (during which Busch, as a corporal, outranked Private Anheuser). Shortly thereafter, Busch bought into the business as junior partner.

Driven principally by the younger man's ambition, the company invested not only in more production facilities but in the infrastructure to expand beyond the local market. A bottling plant utilizing the new pasteurization process and a fleet of refrigerated railroad cars were introduced to bring the beer to distant distributors. The brewers swapped out their subpar suds with a premium recipe from the Bohemian town of Budweis, and promoted it heavily with print ads and posters, promotional deals, and well-paid hype men who splashed cash and bought rounds in taverns across the country. In 1880, when Busch took charge after the passing of his father-in-law,

Adolphus Hotel, Dallas – 1912
1321 Commerce Street

Anheuser-Busch rolled out 141,000 barrels of product, up from just 2,500 barrels in 1862.

Busch was known for his sense of humor and had a reputation as a soft touch. But his generosity was tempered by pragmatism. A close supporter of the mayor, he reliably supplied personal recommendation letters to supplicants seeking a city job. But the mayor knew the secret: Hold the letter up to a light. Only if Busch had poked a pinhole through the eye of the eagle on his corporate letterhead was the recommendation taken seriously. Otherwise, the applicant was told the mayor didn't take orders from some German brewer, no matter how rich.

And rich Busch certainly was. Aside from his St. Louis mansion, he had a winter home in Pasadena with thirty-five acres of meticulously tended gardens—the inspiration for future Busch Gardens theme parks—and a castle in Germany, plus interests in coal, railroads, and hotels. In 1892 he came to Dallas, a southern distribution hub for his spreading national sales network. Busch bought into an upscale hotel in town called the Oriental. Two decades later he built another one across the street.

The luxury Beaux-Arts high-rise with a slate mansard roof and copious ornamentation was more than a match for the toniest properties in Manhattan. So hungry were city fathers for Busch's cash infusion, they tore down city hall to hand him the best parcel. A naming contest heaped on the gratitude, suggesting the edifice be called the Adolphus, and Busch accepted. The St. Louis architectural firm he commissioned for the hotel also was tapped to create a luxury department store and office complex one block away. Originally named the Busch Building, now the Kirby Building, its exterior mimicked the Woolworth Building's Gothic revival style.

Unfortunately, Busch died before he could visit either of his Dallas namesakes. His health had been failing for a while, aggravated by stress brought on by the country's growing temperance movement. He died during a trip to Germany in 1913, less than a year after the Adolphus opened. At least the proud personal friend of Kaiser Wilhelm was spared the wave of anti-German sentiment that arose in his adopted home during World War I. The architects were called back for another project: the Busch mausoleum. His son took over the business, which remained in family control until 2008.

The luxurious hotel has welcomed scores of famous guests, from celebrities to presidents to royalty. But one of the most consequential people to show up at its doors was turned away. In 1955, George Allen, owner of insurance and accounting businesses in the city, arrived by invitation for a meeting, only to be told by the doorman that Blacks were not admitted through the main entrance. The proud businessman refused to use the back door, stubbornly persisting until the other meeting participants finally got the manager to bend the rules. In 1969, Allen became the first Black person elected to the Dallas city council. Eventually they named the county courthouse after him.

The hotel underwent a thorough renovation in recent years, and the concierge gives daily public tours showing off highlights such as the high tea room that for decades also contained a retractable floor and rink for ice dancing revues. An extraordinary carved Steinway that once belonged to the Guggenheim family commands the lounge. Also noteworthy is the large "King of Beers" chandelier that illuminated the Anheuser–Busch display at the 1904 St. Louis World's Fair.

MAGNOLIA BUILDING — Dallas

While the structure is a handsome skyscraper in its own right, it's what's on top of the Magnolia Building that matters most to residents of Dallas. The thirty-foot-tall neon red Pegasus, originally lit up to welcome a conference of the American Petroleum Institute in 1934, has been a symbol of the city ever since.

Would a thirty-foot-tall neon white flower on the roof enjoy the same popularity? That was the original logo of Magnolia Petroleum, the local oil company that built this tower. The founder had named the business after his aunt, a doyenne of Galveston society. But the founder was no longer living when the conference came to town, and his building got the red Pegasus of Mobiloil, the trademark fuel brand of Standard Oil Company of New York, or Socony, which owned Magnolia as a subsidiary.

Magnolia Willis was born and raised on a Texas cotton plantation near Houston that was also called "Magnolia." In 1875, just a few years after her debutante ball, she married her father's business associate, a man twice her age named George Sealy. Sealy and his older brother John were the sons of an Irish blacksmith, and the two had come to Galveston to work in a dry goods business. They had become cotton traders, and during the war their chief concern was getting merchant ships past the Union coastal blockades to sell their cotton in England. In the years since, they had expanded into banking and railroads.

John's son, John Jr., became a full partner in his father's bank upon graduation from Princeton. When a devastating hurricane blasted Galveston in 1900, John Jr. was appointed head of the city finance commission to raise funds to fix the damage. His aunt's stately mansion, "Open Gates," stoutly withstood the storm; true to its name, it temporarily sheltered hundreds of refugees. Magnolia was widowed the following year, and John Jr. stepped in to fill his uncle's shoes as leader of the Sealy interests, including the city wharf and rail line. He also looked after the city hospital, which had been founded through a generous bequest from his father.

An astute businessman with an eye for further investments, Sealy snapped up some oil properties in Corsicana and Beaumont when they were auctioned in the aftermath of an antitrust lawsuit. In 1911 he founded Magnolia Petroleum, and five years later he moved the company to Dallas. In what might have been viewed as an un-neighborly gesture, Sealy shortly set about seizing the title of tallest office tower in Texas from the Adolphus Hotel next door. The design is by British-born architect Alfred Bossom, who also invented an emergency oxygen system for bank employees unfortunate enough to be locked in a vault; the first one was installed in Galveston.

As the Magnolia Building went up in 1921, a newspaper in Snyder, 250 miles west of Dallas, noted accurately if verbosely that "if all the people who in the future will occupy space in the structure were to be taken up bodily and transported to some place on the prairie, they would be sufficient in number to make a town that would surpass in point of population the average town in the State of Texas." The writer closed with an appropriately Texas-sized boast that the building "will stand until the pyramids fall." The next summer, locals crowded the streets to watch a couple minor league fielders try to catch baseballs dropped from the top story.

The tower is now a hotel, and guests on the historically preserved twenty-fourth floor get rooms with full wood paneling that dates from the structure's opening. The skybridge at the nineteenth floor is unfortunately inaccessible to the public, but visitors can appreciate the extravagant original interior in the elevator lobby. Otherwise, most of the décor has been replaced—including Pegasus himself. The beacon lighting up the Dallas skyline now was unveiled on New Year's Day 2000. The restored original is on display outside the convention center.

Magnolia Building, Dallas – 1922
1401 Commerce Street

NEWS TOWER — Miami

Perched atop this pastel yellow tower is a Spanish galleon like the one Ponce de Leon sailed on his first expedition to Florida. It's not the original—both it and the cupola were blown off in a ferocious 1926 hurricane. Fortunately, the owner knew how to recover from a fall. James Cox suffered one of the most humiliating routs in presidential election history, but bounced back to build a media empire.

He grew up on an Ohio farm near Dayton, the youngest of seven children. A brother-in-law owned a small weekly newspaper in Middletown, and Cox practically lived there, working as a reporter, editor, proofreader, bookkeeper, and circulation manager. When a businessman in town who appreciated Cox's gumption got elected to Congress, he hired the young newsman as his secretary. A few years later, he loaned Cox the money to buy the struggling *Dayton Daily News*.

By reinvigorating the newspaper and buying another small one nearby, Cox built enough local influence to win two terms to Congress, then was elected governor of Ohio in 1912. A former teacher, he focused on statewide education reforms and also pushed through the state's first worker's compensation law for people injured on the job. A Democrat in a Republican-leaning state, he lost his first reelection bid to the then two-year term, but won back the governor's mansion in 1916 and kept it two years later. By 1920, the national party picked Cox to succeed the ailing Woodrow Wilson in the White House. Aided by his charismatic young veep nominee, Franklin D. Roosevelt, Cox crusaded in support of Wilson's unpopular League of Nations plan. His Republican opponent was Warren Harding, another Ohio newspaper publisher, who quietly campaigned from his front porch and promised war-weary Americans a "Return to Normalcy." They swept him into office by a historic popular vote landslide margin, nearly two-to-one.

Cox went back to newspapering. He spent the winter in Miami in 1923, and loved it so much that he bought a house in town, plus a local newspaper to keep him busy. The following year, a developer announced plans for a luxury hotel in nearby Coral Gables with a tower modeled after the belfry of a

News Tower, Miami – 1925
600 Biscayne Boulevard

Spanish cathedral. Cox hired the hotel's architect, Leonard Schultze, and had him design a skyscraper also modeled on the same Giralda tower in Seville for the *Miami Daily News*. A third Giralda tower got underway for a Miami Beach hotel, making south Florida's budding skyline more than a bit repetitive.

To celebrate the opening of the News Tower, the paper printed a special 504-page souvenir Sunday edition that must have caused shoulder injuries to south Florida paperboys. It was a big news weekend in the traditional sense as well. On Saturday, directly in front of the News Tower, the boss of a competing paper tried to beat an oncoming train across the railroad tracks. Neither he nor his car survived, and a young woman with him lost a leg. On Sunday, the mayor had a fatal stroke.

The following year, a severe hurricane tore the top off Cox's skyscraper, sending it crashing through the main newsroom below, narrowly missing several editors and reporters covering the storm. It wasn't the worst thing that happened to a Cox newspaper in 1926. The editor of the *Canton Daily News* was murdered by gangsters that year after publishing an expose on city corruption and organized crime. The paper got the Pulitzer for public service, and Cox kept up his chain's reputation for anti-mafia crusades. The *Miami Daily News* regularly tweaked Al Capone, who bought a house on an island in Biscayne Bay. Cox claimed in his autobiography that he once scolded and sent away a well-dressed mafia go-between who had come to his office with a check to buy the paper for an amount far in excess of its value. Cox also confided that he was the one who tipped off the feds to go after "Scarface" for income tax evasion.

In 1962, with the paper having relocated to more modern offices, the federal government took a lease on the property. It was renamed Freedom Tower, and for a decade it was the processing and documentation center for the tens of thousands of Cuban refugees fleeing the revolution on their island. Later that year, the *Daily News* got perhaps the scoop of the twentieth century when it was first to break the story of Soviet missiles in Cuba.

The paper folded in 1988, but Cox's media empire remains. His last surviving child, Anne, lived to one hundred and was the richest person in Georgia when she died in 2020. The building, now part of the regional community college but still called the Freedom Tower, flies a Cuban flag next to the Florida and U.S. standards and contains museum galleries dedicated to the Cuban diaspora in south Florida. The original entryway feels antique and very Spanish with its tile and inlaid wood. Carved scenes of the first printing press are mounted above the elevator doors. In the colonnaded ballroom, formerly the paper's main business and circulation office, a reproduction of an original wall mural commemorates the first European explorers landing in Florida five centuries ago.

Nashville Trust Building, Nashville – 1926
315 Union Street

NASHVILLE TRUST BUILDING — Nashville

An amusing example of skyscraper gamesmanship can be found in the old financial district of Nashville, where two neighboring banks that once raced to be Nashville's tallest building are now joined together as a single hotel. That union is superficial—above street level, none of the floors line up.

The Nashville Trust Building, the ever-so-slightly shorter of the two, was built for an institution founded in 1889 with the financial backing of a distiller and wholesale grocer named Charles Nelson, who was its first president. Nelson came from a family of German immigrants who suffered a catastrophe crossing the Atlantic when a storm swept their father overboard. Worse, he was wearing a money belt stuffed with their savings. Charles worked in a New York candle and soap factory until the family moved to Cincinnati, where he became a butcher and partner in a grocery. Early in the Civil War, occupied Nashville became an important transit hub for supplies. Nelson relocated there and started a grocery wholesaling business. The profits enabled him to buy a distillery in 1870, and that made him rich enough to be approached by the trust company's organizers.

The business mostly handled estates, wills, and trusts at first, though it gradually expanded into savings and checking accounts. In 1903 it opened an impressive two-story building with polished stone columns flanking its entrance. A decade later, the building was enlarged to encompass a brokerage for stocks and bonds. As Nashville grew as a regional financial center, a competitor opened next door on the corner, fronted with a more impressive four-story colonnaded facade. This presumably rankled Charles's son, William, who succeeded his father as president in 1917. A few years later, he announced the construction of a fourteen-story headquarters for Nashville Trust on Union Street, just around the corner behind the bigger American National Bank.

The head of that institution, Paul Davis, had once worked at Nashville Trust; his bank was regarded as an upstart, popular with the "new money" crowd as opposed to his former employer's more established customer base. Davis was not about to allow his bank to be dwarfed. Instead, he hired architects to stack an additional eleven stories on top of his building to snatch the title of tallest skyscraper in Nashville before Nelson could claim it.

Passersby gawked as girders and walls for the two skyscrapers shot up shoulder to shoulder in 1925, setting a speed record for local construction. Bested by an extra floor, Nashville Trust retaliated in its advertisements and postcards by airbrushing their next-door neighbor out of existence. That gesture apparently did not quell the anxieties of Nelson, who had a heart attack less than a year after the skyscraper opened.

Controlling interest in Nashville Trust was purchased by James Caldwell, another banker who had built his initial fortune through the grocery business. Like the senior Nelson, Caldwell had also seen his family lose its wealth suddenly, but under much different circumstances. Caldwell's family was forced to abandon a two-thousand-acre Mississippi cotton plantation in the face of advancing Union troops. In his memoirs, Caldwell recalled how he and his brother tried to make back some of their losses by selling tobacco and cloth to their former slaves at five times markup. The profiteering scheme came to nothing when the Confederate currency they were paid with became worthless.

Caldwell's tenure at Nashville Trust was brief. His son, Rogers, was enjoying mercurial success with his own company as a bond writer for municipal construction projects and corporate expansions. The young man, touted as "the J.P. Morgan of the South," assembled a highly leveraged portfolio of controlling ownership in regional banks, insurance companies, and newspapers. But his position crumbled in the crash, and his financial interests were so enmeshed in his father's bank that it also faced collapse. So Davis's American swooped in and swallowed Nashville Trust and Caldwell's bank. When it spun off the merged trust operations of American and Nashville, the new president was Charles Nelson's grandson.

A historical marker notes that the first American school for seeing eye dogs was briefly headquartered here. Both building's facades are well preserved, and the lobbies of both, while thoroughly remodeled, bear traces of their former appearance.

NIELS ESPERSON BUILDING — Houston

This skyscraper is a woman's tribute to the husband she loved. And Houston has conveniently obliged the handsome bronze Italian Renaissance edifice by placing one of its many mirrored skyscrapers directly across the street—all the better for the Niels Esperson Building to preen.

Mellie Keenan was a teenager when her family left Kansas for the heart of what is now Oklahoma. In territory reserved for indigenous people including the Cherokee who had been relocated in the "Trail of Tears," a large unclaimed area in the center was thrown open to non-Natives in the Sooner land rush of 1889. Mellie's family got a homestead in a place called Yukon, west of Oklahoma City. Something caught her eye there on the prairie: a real estate agent twice her age selling lots in nearby El Reno.

Niels Esperson was a Danish immigrant who had studied geology in California hoping to strike it rich as a gold prospector. When that didn't pan out, he decided to try land speculation in Oklahoma, where he met the love of his life. The couple were married in 1893 and lit out for adventure in Colorado, where a gold rush was on. Not only didn't they turn up any precious metal while draining their savings, but Niels contracted tuberculosis. A staunch Christian Scientist, he refused any medical treatment. Mellie suggested they move back to Kansas, where she had family.

For two years while he recuperated, Niels pored over books and articles about a new method of striking it rich: petroleum. After ten years of marriage, they moved to Houston and borrowed money to drill wells around a salt dome formation in nearby Humble that bore some resemblance to recent big gushers, including Spindletop. Their first four wells were dry, but with the fifth one, the Espersons got lucky. They finally struck it rich.

Their company, Invincible Oil, drilled more than 200 successful wells. With no children, Mellie learned the business alongside Niels, who diversified into real estate, buying a large ranch and rice farms and investing in a ship channel being dredged through the bayou to the Gulf of Mexico. He also planned a luxurious downtown cinema, and hired a Chicago architect, John Eberson, who had made a name for himself with similar projects. This one was to be modeled after an Italian villa, with a ceiling painted sky blue and embedded with twinkling lights to serve as stars when the house lights went down.

They were attending a theater in Chicago on a visit to meet with Eberson in the fall of 1922 when Niels suddenly felt ill. The couple left after the first act and retreated to their hotel, where things only got worse. Niels died shortly after midnight, sixty-five years old.

The theater opened in January. Mellie soon called on Eberson for another project: an office tower Niels had dreamed of building across the street from the cinema. The architect stuck with the Italian Renaissance theme for the tower, and modeled it after the Wrigley Building in Chicago, which Niels admired. Its appropriately theatrical roofline is rich with urns and obelisks and crowned with a cupola covered in gold leaf. At the groundbreaking, Mellie throttled up the steam shovel and dug the first scoops of dirt herself.

The building, dedicated in 1927, became the tallest skyscraper in Texas. Mellie kept offices on the twenty-fifth floor and took tea on a private roof garden. She sold the building the year after it opened, maintaining her office there, then snatched it back during the Depression when it went into default, regaining it for much less than the original cost to construct. A business rival, banker and publisher Jesse Jones, built a nearby Art Deco skyscraper (modeled on Eliel Saarinen's Tribune Tower contest entry) allegedly to block Mellie's view of her ship channel holdings.

The lobby, while altered, retains its marble trim. A bust of Niels watches over the original brass elevator doors, which are decorated with a custom crest featuring the couple's initials and Viking motifs honoring Niels's Scandinavian background. Mellie's portrait hangs in the elevator lobby next door, in the Mellie Esperson Building. Also by Eberson, it was built slightly smaller than her husband's, standing by its side and connected on nearly every floor. But by its opening in 1941, Mellie's vision was gone. She developed cataracts, and as a faithful Christian Scientist like her late husband, she refused medical treatment. He never saw his building, and she never saw hers.

Niels Esperson Building, Houston – 1927
808 Travis Street

6

The West

America held two newspaper skyscraper races in the 1890s. While the *New York Tribune*, the *Sun*, and the *Times* were one-upping their competitors with eye-popping Manhattan headquarters at the foot of the Brooklyn Bridge, three rival publishers on the far side of the continent crowded three high-rises into their own edition of Newspaper Row.

The first skyscraper on the West Coast was an odd-looking affair. Chicagoans Daniel Burnham and John Root designed it for the *San Francisco Chronicle* in 1890, and it was arguably the strangest building they ever produced—an asymmetrically angled ten-story stone mass with an elephantine clock turret plunked on its roof. Five years later, the owners of the *San Francisco Call* revealed their plans for a "marble palace" one hundred feet taller than the Chronicle Building. When the publisher of the *Examiner*, a young Harvard dropout named William Randolph Hearst, failed to persuade his mother to allocate sufficient funds to outdo the others, his paper sniffed that its elegant new seven-story office was superior to heavier structures that "have no proper place in semi-tropic California."

Catastrophe brought the rivals together, if only for one day. On April 19, 1906, a joint edition under the masthead *Call-Chronicle-Examiner* ran one huge headline: "EARTHQUAKE AND FIRE: SAN FRANCISCO IN RUINS." Newspaper Row would never be the same.

CALL. CHRONICLE. MILLS. CROCKER.
HOW "THE CALL" BUILDING WILL COMPARE WITH OTHER HIGH STRUCTURES IN SAN FRANCISCO.

A newspaper illustration from 1895 compares San Francisco's tallest skyscrapers.

The story of the American West is so full of dramatic twists, hidden treasures, and unspeakable tragedies that it can seem more screenplay than actual history. The first settlers who followed the Oregon Trail through the Rocky Mountains risked starving, freezing, drowning in river rapids, or being attacked by the resident population jealously defending their dwindling land. Despite the nationalistic sentiment of "manifest destiny" urging them to spread West until the land ran out, few were willing to take the risk. Travel by sea was hardly more appealing; a ship departing New York needed six months to loop around stormy Cape Horn and up the other coastline.

An 1845 guidebook for Americans considering the journey estimated that California had perhaps one thousand foreign residents. It was part of Mexico then, though not for much longer. In addition to being light on Americans, California had relatively few Mexicans. That proved helpful the next year, when the United States provoked Mexico into a territorial war, and its naval forces in the Pacific easily breezed down the coast and occupied each of the small California settlements without firing a shot. By 1848, treaties with Mexico and Great Britain reset the boundaries of a vast American hinterland. People just needed a reason to go.

Gold turned out to be an excellent draw. With its discovery in the western slopes of the Sierra Nevadas, swarms of fortune-hunters poured into the state in 1849. Subsequent discoveries of gold, silver, and other precious metals in Nevada, Colorado, Arizona, and elsewhere brought more prospectors. Merchants followed in their wake, settlements grew, and cities developed.

Some cities expanded for other reasons. Salt Lake City started as a colony of religious dissidents who sought to leave the United States entirely. Unluckily for them, just as they got to Mexico, its border moved six hundred miles south. Los Angeles was a ranching community until residents traded cattle pens for oil wells. San Diego, then as now, was simply too lovely not to want to live there. But it was mining that settled the West. The last great gold rush in 1896 transformed the remote lumber and fishing port of Seattle into a major supply center for prospectors headed for the Yukon gold fields. The influence of mining showed up even in unexpected places. Underground cables that pull the streetcars up and down San Francisco's hills, for instance, are adapted from cable used to haul ore out of a mineshaft.

Eventually, the United States had to solve the transportation problem. The massive undertaking to build a transcontinental railroad necessitated strong federal government backing, and politicians and railroad officials lining their pockets touched off several embarrassing corruption scandals. It also seeded racial animosity. Four of every five workers who built the tracks through frozen mountain passes and scorching deserts were Chinese immigrants recruited by the railroads. When their job was done, many chose to stay. Tension mounted until the passage in 1882 of the Chinese Exclusion Act. It remains the only time the country has ever barred an entire nationality from its shores, and it presaged further anti-Asian discrimination to come.

Another federally-backed construction project, the Panama Canal, resolved the West's final transportation problem. With work underway in 1904, the business leaders of San Francisco proposed that their city host the next

1915 San Francisco World's Fair

world's fair to celebrate the canal's completion. The 1906 earthquake only stiffened their resolve to hold their Panama-Pacific Exposition.

There was one small hitch five hundred miles down the coast. Business leaders in San Diego had a similar idea for something they were calling the Panama-California Exposition. Neither side relented, and both expositions were held in 1915. Both featured lovely buildings of classical design, though San Diego leaned more heavily on Spanish Baroque and Colonial styles than Beaux-Arts. Both drew good crowds; San Diego even extended its fair a year, and some of the international exhibitors from San Francisco relocated to the grounds at Balboa Park. Presumably it beat returning to Europe, which was embroiled in a brutal war.

The San Francisco and San Diego expositions broke new ground California-style thanks to Hollywood. Producer Mack Sennett sent two of his most bankable comedy stars, Roscoe "Fatty" Arbuckle and Mabel Normand, to shoot at each event. Both silent short films can be found online today, though only one is worth watching. *Fatty and Mabel at the San Diego Exposition* is a slapstick romp, and features a chase scene with one of the fair's electric-powered wicker carts.

* * *

Flood Building, San Francisco – 1904
870 Market Street

FLOOD BUILDING — San Francisco

The immense antique office block that towers over tourists waiting at the Powell Street cable car turntable was built for a man whose rags-to-riches success story is quintessentially San Francisco. The child of Irish immigrants, James Flood went from tending bar to trading stocks to the top tier of West Coast wealth. But even after he was known coast to coast as one of the "Bonanza Kings" of the Comstock Lode, he never forgot his wild side.

Flood was twenty-two and working in a Brooklyn carriage shop in 1849 when, enticed by news of the Gold Rush, he booked passage on a ship for San Francisco. The nuggets he found prospecting amounted to more money than he'd ever seen. Flood went home, married an Irish girl named Emma, bought a farm in Illinois, and moved there with his wife and his parents. But country life did not sit well with him. California was calling.

So James returned with his wife to San Francisco in 1856. He and a convivial fellow Irishman named Billy O'Brien opened a saloon that became a popular lunchtime haunt for stockbrokers from the nearby exchange. Flood was an excellent bartender, and his preferred tips were not coins, but hot tips on which stocks to buy. Investing his money and his partner's, Flood made enough speculating on mining stocks that in 1867 the men opened up their own brokerage.

That's when two more Irishmen, career miners James Fair and John Mackay, approached with a business proposition: They knew of a neglected mine in the Comstock Lode—the country's first major silver discovery, which had been attracting prospectors to western Nevada for a decade. Experience led them to believe it could yield many more tons of valuable ore if mined properly. Could Flood help them to quietly acquire enough shares to win control from the bankers who owned it?

The four created a partnership and did just that. At the next shareholders meeting, they voted out the leadership and made Flood the president of the Hale & Norcross mine. Fair and Mackay were right, and all four got rich. Rather that cashing out, they gambled again on what seemed an even longer shot, stealthily taking over another unproductive mine called the

Consolidated Virginia that Fair felt certain had more silver to give.

Twelve hundred feet underground, threatened by scalding hot springs as well as fires and tunnel collapse, the miners progressed slowly. Pounding away with sledgehammers and spikes by lamplight, they stuffed each hole with blasting powder. At last they found what they wanted: a deposit of pale green ore shot through with silver. The deposit was colossal, like nothing ever seen, before or since. The vein of ore—which in 1873 sold for more than $600 per ton—was six hundred feet deep, two hundred feet wide, and stretched almost a quarter mile. Excited news reports called it the "big bonanza."

It was about then that Flood did something crazy. A New York reporter was in town to write a story about the "Bonanza Kings." He asked where in the scrubland they found enough timber to support all the underground excavation. Flood and Fair rode with him up into the mountains to show off their sawmill near Lake Tahoe and the log flume that brought the wood down to the rail yard below. As a lark, they dared him to ride down to the bottom of the flume with them in a wooden pig trough.

It was the ride of their lives. The flume was seventy feet high in places. Doused and blinded by the spray, the terrified writer gave up trying to gauge his speed and just tried to hang on. Half an hour later, at the end of the fifteen-mile flume, he knew they had averaged thirty miles per hour, faster than a locomotive. But that included comparatively tranquil bits. The fastest sections were as steep as a forty-five degree angle. His story in the *New York Tribune* reported: "Fair said we went at least a mile a minute, Flood said we went at the rate of a hundred miles an hour, and my deliberate belief is that we went at a rate that annihilated time and space." Flood announced he would never do it again, not for the whole Consolidated Virginia mine, which produced enough precious metal to build a full-size replica of Trinity Church entirely made of silver.

The brick and sandstone skyscraper, built years after Flood's death by his son, is still owned by his descendants. It survived the earthquake and fire, as did Flood's brownstone mansion on Nob Hill, now home of the ultra-exclusive Pacific Union Club. But the Flood Building almost fell to the wrecking ball in 1950. Woolworth's had a department store on the ground floor, and had a deal to purchase the building and tear it down for a new store when the federal government stepped in, requisitioning the warren of office space for various agencies during the Korean War.

The boomerang-shaped gray marble lobby has patterned floors, red granite columns, and display cases packed with interesting artifacts such as a charred beam from the 1906 fire. Dashiell Hammett, author of the Sam Spade detective novels, worked as a Pinkerton agent in the Flood Building and set the final scene of *The Maltese Falcon* at the grill next door. Flood's great-grandson, Jim, considered the building a family heirloom and spent millions repairing damage from a Woolworth modernization of the original exterior, replacing its entryway arches. He died of a heart attack in 2020 at the age of eighty after a day of skiing in Jackson Hole, Wyoming. Considering the log flume, adventure runs in the family.

Braly Building, Los Angeles – 1904
408 South Spring Street

BRALY BUILDING — Los Angeles

Elegantly decorated though it may be, little about this office tower suggests it was once the tallest building in Los Angeles. More surprisingly, the skyscraper that surpassed it—the Art Deco city hall four blocks north—was designed by the same architect who created the Braly Building.

John Braly came to the West Coast when his father got so sick that his doctor ordered him to relocate somewhere with milder weather. The family sold the farm in Missouri, herded up the cattle, and joined a wagon train on the Oregon Trail. They narrowly escaped a massacre at a rest stop in present day Washington, departing ten days before the local Cayuse tribe attacked the camp and slaughtered fourteen people. Arriving in Sacramento at the front end of the 1849 Gold Rush, Braly and his father piled the wagon with flour, bacon, beans, picks, and shovels and immediately set out for the mining camps. They made a handsome profit—paid not in coins or bills, but strictly gold dust—and repeated the one-week trip several times to build up their savings.

The family started a farm near Santa Clara, and Braly went back east to college in Tennessee. When he returned, he got married and took a job heading a boarding school. Three years later, he left that job to gamble on loan sharking at a mining encampment in eastern Nevada. That scheme left him broke and humiliated, riding his mule back through the desert to rejoin his wife, Martha, and their baby daughter, Josephine. Martha forgave him, and they both got jobs teaching until John got better offers, first as superintendent of schools in Santa Clara, then as vice president of a college in San Jose.

Nearing fifty, the Bralys decided they had one more shot at making real money, so they moved north to Fresno to start a small bank and a hundred-acre raisin farm. Trained greyhounds kept the jackrabbits at bay, but a serious infestation of worms threatened to ruin their crop. Braly heard turkeys were the only solution—a good-sized bird could eat a hundred worms every day. He immediately bought all the turkeys he could, close to a thousand, and set them loose on the vines. Once the Braly farm was picked clean, he rented out his turkey troops to other farmers. The bank prospered too, and they opened two more. But their Josephine fell ill and died. Another daughter, Millie, also got sick, so the Bralys sold their farm and moved to San Diego, hoping the climate change would help. It didn't.

At the moment they should have been enjoying their burgeoning wealth, the couple had lost two of their five children. Then their son Arthur came down with typhoid. Desperate, they bought a cattle ranch in Arizona and sent him to manage it. He recovered, but his father was shattered. He went to a doctor and received more bad news, which Braly recounted in his memoirs: "After an examination he pronounced me a worn out businessman, adding the comfortable assurance that my hold on life would be one of not more than six months' duration."

So Braly resolved to buy one more bank and set it up for his son to run. He took a majority position in Southern California Savings Bank in Los Angeles and became president. And didn't die. Together with Arthur, he guided the institution through downturns to eventual prosperity, staying with it fifteen years. The directors voted to build a twelve-story office building, and in gratitude to their top executive, named it after him.

The skyscraper, which has changed names several times and is now loft apartments, was the first for its architect, an Englishman named John Parkinson. He went on to design more buildings up and down Spring Street, including all four standing a block south of the Braly at the intersection with Fifth Street. None equaled the height of his original, simply because the Braly Building's construction led the city to enact a lower height limit. However, the rule did not restrict government buildings, allowing Parkinson finally to top his first skyscraper with his last, Los Angeles City Hall.

After retirement, John and Martha Braly threw themselves into political activism on behalf of women's suffrage. They hosted fundraising banquets and drove across the state campaigning, which earned Braly the title "father of California women's suffrage." But he refused another honorific, rebuffing founders of a town in the Imperial Valley who tried to name it after him. Instead they called it Brawley—which, incidentally, is how Braly's name is pronounced.

MERCHANTS EXCHANGE — San Francisco

San Francisco today has few signs of the earthquake that left the city in ruins and killed three thousand residents. Most of the damage was repaired more than a century ago. But the cracks that creep up the forty-foot columns at the Merchants Exchange entryway show the power of the tremor that once laid waste to this city and left half its people homeless.

Merchants exchanges were once a fixture of port cities. Retailers, whole-salers, and suppliers could learn the latest shipping news and make deals there. In the days before wireless transmission from ships at sea, knowing when a vessel was due to arrive and what cargo it carried was essential for traders. Ships conveyed this information via signal flags even before arrival at the wharf, and the contents of their holds might be entirely sold before the stevedores began unloading. This building, the city's third merchants exchange, has a lookout tower on the roof to track ships arriving through the Golden Gate. It also was a meeting place for other business associations, including the chamber of commerce and agricultural exchange.

In 1900, members felt the time had arrived to replace their five-story Victorian structure with a fifteen-story skyscraper. They hired the Chicago firm of Daniel Burnham, who delegated the job to his top California archi-tect, Willis Polk. Shipping magnate William Babcock, the president of the exchange, laid the cornerstone in 1903. At the dedication ceremonies two years later, a federal judge marveled that the building looked like someone had "sailed a great ocean liner ... up California Avenue and set her on end." From the speakers table, Babcock bubbled with optimism. "Let us greet the new California which is springing into existence," he exhorted.

When the earthquake came, its epicenter was only two miles off the coastline. San Francisco caught the brunt of it, but people felt vibrations as far away as Oregon, Nevada, and Los Angeles. The exchange building was sturdy enough to survive the vibrations intact, as were several other of the city's skyscrapers. But most of them, including the exchange, were gutted by the fires that swept through the city. It had to be stripped back down to its steel skeleton in many places and rebuilt.

Meanwhile across the bay, Oakland also suffered significant earthquake damage, but no widespread fires. Inspectors were therefore surprised to discover that a seventy-foot bell tower at Mills College, built of still-experimental reinforced concrete, had survived the quake unscathed. Its designer, a native San Franciscan named Julia Morgan, had just two years earlier become the first female architect licensed in the state's history. After studying architecture at Paris's École des Beaux-Arts—also the first woman to do so—she had opened her first office in San Francisco in 1904, less than a block away from the Merchants Exchange.

With its impressive display of durability under duress, the bell tower won Morgan numerous post-earthquake commissions, including an interior redesign and rebuild of the Merchants Exchange. She moved her office to its thirteenth floor, where it remained for the rest of her remarkable career. Morgan's talent in drafting and design was balanced by a thorough understanding of engineering and materials. She was also fiercely protective of her clients' privacy—and her own. Now widely assumed to have been a lesbian, Morgan wore trousers instead of skirts and was eager to get her hands dirty on job sites. When masonry workers were repairing cracks in the exchange building's terracotta cornice, she climbed up onto the scaffolding to review the work. After coming back down the ladder, her gray suit spattered with mortar and wide-brimmed hat knocked askew, she encouraged her junior draftsman to do likewise.

The new lobby featured a barrel-vaulted ceiling and skylight illuminating the marble columns and archways, composing a space that induces awe to this day. Morgan commissioned six huge murals of shipping and maritime scenes for the trading hall; they can be seen in the space, now a bank. The magnificent, mahogany-paneled ballroom has been named in honor of Morgan and has been a preferred venue for ultra-swanky wedding receptions and similarly ritzy to-dos for more than a century. One of the first was a black-tie gala at the Merchants Exchange to raise the funds to pay for the 1915 San Francisco World's Fair.

Merchants Exchange, San Francisco – 1905
465 California Street

U.S. Grant Hotel, San Diego - 1910
326 Broadway

U.S. GRANT HOTEL — San Diego

Being the son of a president can be a heavy burden—surely even more so if your father also won the Civil War. Considering that Ulysses S. Grant Jr. showed his gratitude by steering his father into a Ponzi scheme that ruined them both, one can understand why he moved to the other side of the country.

President Grant's oldest child, who went by "Buck," attended Harvard and Columbia Law School during his father's eight years in office. He served as his father's personal White House secretary before becoming an assistant U.S. attorney in New York. In 1880, Buck bought into lending his famous name to an investment partnership with Ferdinand Ward, who turned out to be a Wall Street swindler. Grant and his dad each sank $100,000 in the venture, called Grant & Ward, and encouraged many others to do the same. When it went south, the former president borrowed another $150,000 from William Vanderbilt to try to bail out Buck and lost that too. Then he was diagnosed with terminal throat cancer.

That set the stage for a final display of the general's heroism, this time for his family. Grant pushed through the agony and rushed to complete his memoirs, which his friend Mark Twain agreed to publish. He died five days after handing in the manuscript, which became a best seller—hailed then, as it is now, with nearly universal acclaim. It made a fortune for his widow and children, including Buck, who had married Fannie Chaffee, the only daughter of a wealthy senator. She had health problems, so in 1893, in search of a gentler climate, the family moved to San Diego.

They invested in real estate there. Fannie bought San Diego's original hotel, built by city founder Alonzo Horton, and deeded it to her husband, who had it demolished in 1905 to make way for a hotel to be named after his dad. To design it, Buck picked Harrison Albright, a California architect who specialized in hotels. The man had made a name for himself with a spa resort in West Baden Springs, Indiana, which had a multistory atrium sheltered by the world's biggest freestanding dome. Unfortunately, the San Francisco earthquake the following year caused delays, as construction crews flocked north to aid in the rebuilding effort. Financial problems arose. The steel skeleton stood unfinished for three years. Fannie died.

Getting the project over the line required an infusion of cash. It came from investors led by G. Aubrey Davidson, a banker and president of the chamber of commerce. Davidson was also the top proponent of holding an exposition in San Diego to celebrate the opening of the Panama Canal, and he knew the Grant's five hundred rooms would be crucial to its success. Another investor shelled out extra for a lighted fountain in the park across the street. Though a luxury property, the hotel leaned hard on military themes and gimmicks, including tent encampments on the rooftop and a dining room called the Bivouac Grill decorated with murals of famous Civil War battles. Atop the grand staircase hung an oil portrait of the beloved president.

Buck was out of town and missed the 1910 opening, though he sent a congratulatory telegram. For a time, he headed the Panama-California Exposition; at the groundbreaking ceremonies, his hotel hosted a banquet and a ball. By the time the expo opened in Balboa Park, Davidson was in charge. Eventually U.S. Grant Jr. remarried, finding love again with a widowed socialite whose incredible name was even more patriotic than his own: America Workman Will. They moved into the hotel and lived out the rest of their lives there.

Renovations over the years altered the lobby and covered a landscaped patio that used to look out over the bay, but the painting of Grant is still there. The hallways are lined with historic artifacts documented in a self-guided tour brochure available from the concierge. It does not mention that in 1970 the hotel hosted the first San Diego Comic-Con, the world's biggest annual gathering of Superman aficionados. But it does explain the portraits of several esteemed members of the local Sycuan tribe, which has owned the hotel since 2003.

DANIELS & FISHER TOWER — Denver

Framed against the Rocky Mountains, this ornamental office tower was for decades a symbol of the Mile High City. Originally offices for Denver's premier department store, it was built by the founder's son, whose attention to the family retail business never matched his yearning for adventure and travel. But loyal to the end, he ordered an urn with his ashes be kept in the store after he died.

William Daniels was running dry goods stores in Iowa and Kansas when the Colorado gold rush prompted him to open one in Denver, selling clothes and equipment to the prospectors and miners. His new branch succeeded, and in 1872 a former clerk from his Iowa establishment, William Fisher, joined the business as a partner. They employed a small army of seamstresses making store brand clothes, one of whom, Margaret Tobin, later became famous as the "Unsinkable Molly Brown."

Daniels's only child, William, was an unruly brat. Kicked out of three Denver schools for setting fires, he was sent away to boarding school. After graduating from Yale, he briefly worked as a cub reporter in New York, then sailed to Japan in 1890 to study Buddhism. While there, he got word that his father had died. So the young man returned to Denver and worked with the surviving partner for seven years, until Fisher died. Fully in control but hungry for adventure, he volunteered for the Spanish-American War and put an old newspaper pal in charge of the business.

When Daniels returned to Denver, he published a short book, *The Department Store System*, pointing out that customers preferred to shop "amid beautiful and even artistic surroundings." He enjoyed duck hunting—to excess, bagging more than a thousand waterfowl in one two-week Utah excursion. By 1902, no longer able to stave off his wanderlust, Daniels sailed for South America, ostensibly hunting for gold and diamonds. His wife, Edith, stayed behind in Denver. He didn't come back for five years, and after a while she divorced him for desertion.

From South America, Daniels went to England, where he learned of a planned anthropological expedition to New Guinea to be undertaken by the London Geographical Society. He offered to bankroll it if he could join. The crew sailed for Australia, where Daniels was quickly smitten with a beautiful English noblewoman, Cicely Banner. She agreed to stick around while he conducted his scientific voyage. A mutual Australian friend, Florence Martin, let Banner stay with her. Like Daniels, Martin was a child of privilege who dreamed of being a scientist; she had spent a year in Cambridge as a physics research student. After sixteen months, Daniels and his colleagues finished their exploration and brought back a trove of tools, weapons, musical instruments, and ornaments, some of which are now on display in the British Museum. The lovestruck couple returned to England and were married in 1907. Martin came too, and moved in with them, splitting time between their English manor, a chateau they rented in France, and occasionally, Colorado.

Wishing to decisively distinguish Daniels & Fisher from its competitors, the heir commissioned a replica of St. Mark's Campanile to become the store's centerpiece. The original in Venice was in the news at the time, being rebuilt after a 1902 collapse. Daniels duplicated its forty-foot width, but purposely made his version one foot taller. When completed, it was the tallest building west of the Mississippi, and its observation deck became a sightseeing destination. Doubling down on the height gimmick, the store hired a seven-foot-tall doorman.

Both Daniels and his young wife died in 1918 in the global influenza pandemic. The business was left to the manager, while the remainder of the estate went to Martin, who moved to Denver and became a philanthropist. In the 1950s, a New York developer bought Daniels & Fisher and relocated it to a modern shopping complex designed by a young architect named I.M. Pei. The older store was torn down (so was Pei's store eventually), but the tower survived. A radio station took up residence for a few years, and each day the deejay faithfully climbed a ladder up its disused elevator shaft to wind the clock mechanism.

The tower underwent an extensive renovation in time for New Year's Eve celebrations in 2000. A historical exhibit on the ground floor includes interesting photos from the old store. The upper floors, including the space behind the four huge glass clock faces, can be rented out for parties.

Daniels & Fisher Tower, Denver – 1911
1601 Arapahoe Street

HEARST BUILDING — San Francisco

Perhaps this Spanish-influenced office tower should be nicknamed "Rose-bud." Just as the childhood sled opened a window into the tortured psyche of *Citizen Kane*, this Spanish-influenced antique skyscraper holds a key to understanding William Randolph Hearst, the inspiration for Charles Foster Kane. But unlike the sled in the movie, this building never belonged to the famous multimillionaire media baron, he of the spectacular castle and thwarted political ambitions. It was his mom's.

Phoebe Apperson was a primary schoolteacher in Missouri when she met George Hearst, a miner twice her age who had returned to his hometown to care for his dying mother. Married and soon pregnant at the age of twenty, Phoebe moved with him back to San Francisco in 1862. While George was working in mining camps in the hinterlands, Phoebe raised their only child, hoping to mold William into a smart, sophisticated heir to the family fortune. When he was ten, she took him on an eighteen-month tour of Europe. The attention she lavished on her son did not preclude Phoebe—or as some called her, "the Empress"—from devoting herself to other worthy causes. She donated funds and led volunteer efforts to restore Mount Vernon and build kindergartens and YWCAs in the West, and was the first woman to sit on the board of regents at the University of California in Berkeley.

College didn't agree with William, who got into Harvard but socialized too much. His favorite campus pastimes were throwing parties and working as the business manager of the *Harvard Lampoon*, the student-run humor magazine. His father had purchased a struggling Democratic newspaper, the *San Francisco Examiner*, a few years earlier in order to build his political influence in the hope of becoming a senator. That strategy worked, and when George Hearst took the oath of office in 1887, the paper got a new name on the masthead: "W.R. Hearst, Proprietor." The upstart publisher had assiduously studied New York's most successful newspapers, and he had grand plans for his. Those desires were only magnified when a rival built San Francisco's first skyscraper for the *Chronicle*. "How long do you suppose it will be before we can put up a building," William wrote to his father, "a stunner that will

Hearst Building, San Francisco – 1911
5 Third Street

knock his endways and make him as sick as he is now making me?"

When Senator Hearst gave the nod, William bought a hotel across Market Street from the Chronicle and trumpeted plans to replace it with a skyscraper. But the plan hit a roadblock when his father died in 1891 and left every penny to Phoebe, who tightened her purse strings to match her apron strings. The planned twelve stories were scaled back to seven, though the Spanish Colonial edifice that opened in 1898 was nevertheless a lavishly ornamented jewel box.

By that time, it hardly mattered. William had bigger fish to fry. Ensconced on the East Coast, he was slugging it out with *New York World* publisher Joseph Pulitzer, poaching the bigger paper's editorial staff and its most popular cartoon, "The Yellow Kid," for Hearst's own *New York Journal*. As his paper clamored for war with Spain over the sinking of the battleship Maine in Havana harbor, its jingoistic tone got a nickname: "yellow journalism." For Hearst, the sensationalism was calculated; like his father, he hoped to use his media to propel himself to higher office. At first, grateful Democratic pols got him elected to Congress in 1902. But when the Tammany machine thwarted Hearst in a bid for New York mayor in 1905, he responded by throwing his hat in the ring for the next year's gubernatorial elections.

An editor at his Chicago newspaper was the first to telephone Hearst with news of a serious earthquake in San Francisco. Hearst advised him not to overplay it; earthquakes were common in his hometown, he explained. Then he went back to bed. Later, when the scale of the damage was clear, Hearst resolved to rebuild. With the paper printing in temporary quarters, he unveiled plans to raise the tallest skyscraper in the West, a twenty-three story giant with a copper belfry on the roof. But Phoebe balked at the cost again, and William had to whittle his dream skyscraper down to half its intended height to get her to pay for it. He contented himself with announcing that its foundation and frame were strong enough to tack another ten stories on top at some indeterminate time in the future.

Meanwhile, he was done running for office. The 1906 New York gubernatorial campaign flamed out after President Theodore Roosevelt let it be known he held Hearst personally responsible for the assassination of William

McKinley. Like other Hearst critics, the president blamed the ferocious anti-government cast of Hearst's newspapers for bringing anarchist assassins out of the woodwork.

Besides two Hearst Buildings, Phoebe bankrolled several other major construction projects in the Bay Area. One involved an international competition to design a campus plan for Berkeley, with a school of mining as its centerpiece to be named after her husband. The winner, a French architect, declined to get involved with the construction, which was handled by a professor of architecture on campus. He was aided by a talented Cal engineering alumna just back from six years of architecture study in Paris, who helped out with drafting the mines building and also designed and managed the construction of a Greek outdoor auditorium. Impressed, Phoebe hired the architect, Julia Morgan, to build her ninety-two-room mansion in Pleasanton and a two-story playhouse for her grandsons. That wasn't the biggest property the boys would get from their grandma: When Phoebe died in the influenza pandemic, most of the inheritance went to her son, but she gave the Hearst Building to her grandsons.

Now with money apparently no object, Hearst asked Morgan to design a women's gymnasium for the Berkeley campus to honor his mother. Then he had an even bigger project for her. Morgan spent the next two decades designing and overseeing the construction of Hearst Castle on family ranch land in the hills above a small whaling village called San Simeon. She also remodeled the lobby of the Hearst Building in 1938, adding gold leaf panels in the entry, a decorative ceiling, bronze medallions with animal designs over the doors, and a shield with a capital "H" for the facade. All are lovely, though in fairness, the original carved marble in the lobby was already stupendous, and Morgan wisely left it alone. The Hearst Corporation continues to own the building—though not the *Examiner*, which it sold after acquiring the *Chronicle*. Plans are underway to convert the antique skyscraper into a boutique hotel.

Walker Bank Building, Salt Lake City – 1912
175 South Main Street

WALKER BANK BUILDING — Salt Lake City

Were it not for a modern skyscraper diplomatically blocking their view, the sculpted eagles on this tower's observation platform would peer directly into the face of the golden angel Moroni atop the steeple of the Salt Lake Temple two blocks away. Considering the friction between the family responsible for this building and the Church of Jesus Christ of Latter-day Saints, it is probably not a coincidence.

The Walker brothers of Yorkshire, England, came to Utah after their father, a formerly prosperous wool merchant, blew the nest egg on bad railroad stocks. When Matthew Walker learned of a religious community in the New World where he could have a fresh start, he decided to become a Mormon. In 1850 he sent his wife and six children on a ship ahead of him while he settled affairs. They met months later in St. Louis, only to discover he had contracted tuberculosis on the voyage. He was dead within a year, and then both girls fell ill with cholera. After burying their father and sisters, the four Walker brothers—Sharp, Rob, Fred, and Matt—begged their disconsolate mother to finish the journey. Rob got cholera on the trail, but she saved him by forcing him to drink salt water. The weary family finally traversed the Wasatch Mountains to the young settlement on the range's western slope.

The eldest son, Sharp, set up a small farm, while Rob and Fred joined a crew digging the foundations for the temple. When they lined up for their payment, they were left empty-handed. Church officials explained that tithing and deferred costs of their passage by ship was deducted from compensation owed. The teens were irked, even more so after Rob risked his life volunteering in a posse to protect settlers from hostile Paiutes and again received not a cent for his trouble. The Walkers stopped attending services and went to work for another English convert who ran a dry goods business.

Tensions between Mormon settlers and the federal government in the fraught years preceding the Civil War led President James Buchanan to send in troops. Camp Floyd, forty-three miles south of Salt Lake City, proved to be a boon. It garrisoned five thousand potential customers with cash to spend, and the brothers opened a store nearby in 1859. They acquired a safe, and

Matt, at fifteen, became the first teller of Walker Brothers Bank. When the Confederates took Fort Sumter, the soldiers were urgently needed back East, so the feds shed their supplies in a huge clearance sale. The Walkers bought all they could haul: lumber, picks, shovels, canned rations, and coffee. It stocked the shelves of their first store in Salt Lake City.

While the Walkers were nominally LDS members and continued writing checks to the church's emigration fund, that was not good enough for Brigham Young. The leader demanded the traditional ten percent. When his emissary showed up at their door, they gave him a check for five hundred dollars. He returned with word from the leader that it would not suffice, so they tore it up in his face and declared that they were no longer Mormon. Young excommunicated the Walkers and ordered the faithful not to shop in their store—though they continued to admit devoted customers through a rear entrance. The church organized a competing store, Zion's Co-operative Mercantile Institution, which ate into the Walker dry goods revenues. But by that point, they had diversified. Their ownership stake in a silver mine yielded a payoff that protected them from the vicissitudes of retail.

Flush with victory, the Walkers purchased a block and built four mansions on it for themselves and their families. They built an opera house for the city and helped to establish the Liberal party, through which so-called "gentiles" hoped to counter Mormon theocracy. On Sabbath days they sailed on the Great Salt Lake to goad their former co-religionists. But the familial bonds eventually fractured. Sharp became an alcoholic and inveterate gambler. Fred married a woman who believed she had supernatural powers, and their occult talk alienated the others until the couple left for San Francisco. When Rob died in 1901, the last brother, Matt, became president of the bank and let Rob's children have the store.

Matt lived long enough to see the family skyscraper. Ads at its opening promised potential tenants the "most conspicuous office building in Salt Lake." A radio tower placed on the roof in 1947 made it even more conspicuous, until it was removed in 1983. It was restored in 2008, and its illuminated letters change color according to the weather.

OAKLAND CITY HALL — Oakland

Colloquially known as "Mayor Mott's wedding cake," this city hall skyscraper seems almost good enough to eat, with white granite walls artistically drizzled with terracotta icing. Frank Mott did much for his city, and he was not afraid to speak his mind, going so far as to ask the public if someone could please think up a better name for Oakland. But when the 1906 earthquake tested his mettle, Mott responded with aplomb.

The oldest of six, Mott was born in San Francisco, but his family moved to Oakland when he was two after his father got a job with the railroad. Organizers had scrapped as too costly the original plan to lay tracks around the bay's southern end, so Oakland became the transcontinental terminus, with ferry service to San Francisco. Mott's father died when the boy was eleven, so he left school to work for the family, first as a telegraph messenger boy, then a telephone operator, and then at a hardware store, which he eventually bought from the owner. In 1895, the mayor appointed Mott to fill a vacancy on city council. He ran for mayor a decade later, and although he had both the Republican and Democratic endorsements, Mott still had to face three opponents. Among Mott's defeated rivals was Jack London, the famous adventure writer and vocal Socialist.

The 1906 earthquake hit Oakland hard enough to leave rubble in the streets. Mott immediately ordered the public not to use furnaces or boilers until chimneys could be inspected for damage. Through prudence and good fortune, the city managed to avoid the fires that doomed San Francisco. But it was inundated with San Franciscans, as an estimated 150,000 refugees poured into a city whose population was only half that size. Governor George Pardee, the former Oakland mayor who had appointed Mott to city council, set up temporary quarters in his old office, sharing space with his successor. Pardee oversaw relief efforts across the bay while Mott made sure the refugees had food and water. Tens of thousands wound up staying permanently.

Mott supported an ultimately fruitless effort to combine the cities of Berkeley, Oakland, and Alameda, and suggested a better name was in order. "Personally I have never thought that the name 'Oakland' was dignified and

City Hall, Oakland – 1914
1 Frank H. Ogawa Plaza

distinctive enough for such as city as we now have," he said. The suggestion unsurprisingly elicited a blast of sarcastic ridicule on the editorial page of the *Oakland Tribune*: "Oakland would not sound so badly in connection with Nott, and Lott, and Rott, and Pott, and Stott, and Fott, and Hott, and Tott, and Swott, and Dott, and Jott, and Slott, and Bott, or even Shott. But Mott! Perish the idea!"

Still, the mayor enjoyed strong public support, particularly after wresting control of the waterfront and port from the railroad. When he advocated for a new city hall skyscraper, voters backed the bond measure by a twelve-to-one margin. With construction underway, the mayor unexpectedly married a Berkeley schoolteacher, and city hall got its matrimonial moniker.

The skyscraper had all the appurtenances of a modern civic building: courtrooms, police and fire offices, various municipal offices, a medical ward, and behind the slit windows lining the top floor beneath the clock tower, jail cells. Elegant, high-ceilinged council chambers open out onto the mezzanine level through giant oak doors. High above the main lobby, the original chandeliers resemble large mirrored disco balls. The exterior ornamentation of figs, grapes, and olives pays homage to the region's rich agricultural bounty.

In his ten years in office, Mott expanded city parks and dredged the tidal basin known as Lake Merritt, inaugurated a civil service system, reorganized the police and fire departments, and established the first city museum. He retired from politics in 1915 and went into real estate development. Two years later, Jack London died, and his widow planted a ceremonial oak tree in front of city hall where he used to perform his soapbox oratories. It is there to this day.

Built of reinforced concrete to be earthquake proof, the skyscraper suffered severe structural damage in the 1989 Loma Prieta tremor. The people of Oakland were not willing to give up their cake. Instead, the building was retrofitted with a new steel skeleton and placed on a modern floating foundation that allows some shifting in the event of another major quake. The jail cells, unoccupied since the 1960s, are now used for storing holiday decorations and other attic-worthy things.

SMITH TOWER — Seattle

Skyscrapers often play fast and loose with the facts, but few can match the bombast of Seattle's Smith Tower. Even before it was built, it was touted as being forty-two stories tall. It still claims it is, though anyone with eyes can count the windows and see it is not. Skeptics might also refer to the number 35 on the button for the top floor observatory—that is, if the friendly elevator operator doesn't distract them. Smith Tower has its original lift cages, one of many reasons it is the best antique skyscraper in the country to visit. Fittingly, for tech-savvy Seattle, it was built by a maker of revolutionary office technology: typewriters.

Lyman Smith came late to the QWERTY party. The son of an upstate New York sheepskin tanner whose business suddenly went baaad, Smith and his older brother partnered with a Syracuse shotgun manufacturer, William Baker, in 1877. Smith married the wealthy mayor's daughter Flora the following year, bought out his partners, and brought his three younger brothers on board. Meanwhile, a competing upstate arms maker, Remington, had begun to expand its product line by manufacturing sewing machines and, in 1873, the first mechanical typewriter. When one of Smith's employees came up with a design with two sets of keys for capital and lowercase letters, the brothers launched their own typewriter company and got out of the shotgun business.

In 1888, Flora went on a West Coast trip with their son, Burns. They came back raving about Seattle, so Smith invested in several downtown parcels sight unseen. Life in Syracuse was rosy—they lived in an impressive mansion, and his business portfolio included a bank, several Great Lakes shipping businesses and a shipyard, and steel and cement companies. He gave Syracuse University a founding donation for a school of engineering, and spent his leisure time yachting, hunting, and collecting orchids.

He finally got around to viewing his western holdings during a visit to the Alaska-Yukon-Pacific Exposition, better known as the 1909 Seattle World's Fair. While there, Smith told the newspaper he would build an eighteen-story skyscraper in town. But when he got back home, his son suggested he shoot

Smith Tower, Seattle – 1914
506 Second Avenue

for the stars—and the free publicity—by making his building much taller than anything else on the West Coast. Weeks after word got out that his building would exceed forty stories, Lyman Smith died, and Burns, who was his father's secretary, took over the project. The Syracuse architects who designed it had never done a skyscraper; their blueprint draws heavily on New York's Woolworth and Singer buildings.

At the opening, Burns proudly gave tours of the top floor observatory, which was opulently decorated as a Chinese temple with teakwood beams and porcelain medallions on the ceiling. He returned to Syracuse afterward and took over his uncle's iron works, manufacturing wheels for trucks. The typewriter company was bought by New York investors and in 1926 merged with a competitor to form Smith-Corona.

The tower's several owners over the years include Ivar Haglund, a legendary Seattle character known for his seafood restaurant, Ivar's Acres of Clams, and his penchant for corny poems and publicity stunts. Resisting his urge to rename the building the "Ivar-y Tower," Haglund instead flew a sixteen-foot salmon windsock from the spire. That triggered a skirmish with city building inspectors until they decided it was a lost cause. A hearing examiner gave her ruling in Haglundesque doggerel: "So no rules were bent, the hearing wasn't a sham/The variance is granted, so Ivar, keep clam."

That was not the last rhyme about it. Death Cab for Cutie's Ben Gibbard wrote an entire song about it, "Teardrop Windows." The title refers to the oddly shaped portals in the pyramidal cap, which once concealed a water tank but now holds a converted penthouse. Even those extra floors don't get Smith Tower to forty-two stories. But visitors will be too happy to quibble after touring its family-friendly museum, enjoying the gorgeous onyx and marble lobby, riding an elevator driven by an actual person while each floor whooshes past the glass doors, munching tapas and sipping cocktails in the exquisite Chinese observatory—and most importantly, gazing at jaw-slackening views from the wraparound outdoor deck, with Puget Sound below, mountains that stretch across the horizon to the east and west, and if the clouds permit, majestic Mount Rainier.

EDISON BUILDING — Los Angeles

If anyone today recognizes the name Sid Grauman, inevitably it is for his most lasting Hollywood contribution: the celebrity handprints and footprints at Grauman's Chinese Theater. Red carpets and waving searchlights were also signature trademarks of the legendary showman. But they fall short of conveying the pageantry of a premiere night at his first L.A. movie house, the 2,300-seat Million Dollar Theatre, where "silent" films were accompanied by a thirty-piece house orchestra and thundering pipe organ.

Grauman was born in Indianapolis, but his family moved quite a bit thanks to his father, David, whose string of odd jobs included organizing the occasional theatrical production. During the Yukon Gold Rush, David and Sid set up a cabaret in an Alaskan mining camp and hired a struggling writer named Jack London to pass out handbills. Father and son next opened a theater in San Francisco called the Unique. When the earthquake wrecked it, they put up a revival preacher's tent with benches and a sign out front: "Nothing to fall on you except canvas." Sid had an eye for talent; a singing waiter who impressed him agreed to perform for the Graumans, and thus began the meteoric career of comedy film star Roscoe "Fatty" Arbuckle.

More theaters opened, first in San Francisco, San Jose, Stockton, and Sacramento, then one in New York City. Sid earned a reputation for putting on lively shows with eye-catching promotions, such as a lightbulb marquee four stories tall. "Showmanship is like any other merchandising: You must first buy desirable material, then present it to attractive advantage, and price it right," he told an interviewer years later. "Above all, you must let the whole world know what you have to sell." He started looking for an opportunity in Los Angeles, and one came with the construction of a twelve-story headquarters for Southern California Edison. The owner was Homer Laughlin Jr., heir to a West Virginia ceramics fortune and owner of the city's first reinforced concrete office building on the lot next door. The new tower at Broadway and Third was decorated in an extremely baroque Spanish style. It had a palatial cinema at sidewalk level, which the Graumans leased.

As managing director of what he called the Million Dollar Theatre, Sid got to work planning an opening night extravaganza. He had a full house for the premiere, including Cecil B. DeMille, D.W. Griffith, Mary Pickford, Douglas Fairbanks, and Charlie Chaplin, as well as the mayor, the chief of police, and leading businessmen eager for the success of the downtown attraction. The feature, a forty-five-minute Western appropriately titled *The Silent Man*, was only a small part of the program—there was also a newsreel, a slapstick comedy, a medley of patriotic war songs performed by the orchestra, a solo by an opera diva, and an organ recital. After the movie ended, its star, William Hart, took to the stage to share stories of his pre-film days as an honest-to-goodness genuine cowboy.

Grauman personally conceived and directed an elaborate prologue each week with a theme and set design related to the feature film. For one vignette, soldiers charged out of trenches in a simulacrum of the Western Front; in another, a farm was recreated on the large stage with a pair of stray cats looking for mice in the hay bales. There were dance numbers—such as one where sixty usherettes in cadet uniforms marched a parade drill on a grand staircase—and endless variety acts, ranging from bird calls to a contest between two teams of autoworkers racing to be the first to build a complete Ford Model T on stage.

A perfectionist and an insomniac, Grauman rehearsed his prologues to the edge of opening night and was known for making 2 a.m. phone calls to his leading actors. His artistic skills with dramatic lighting and set design were matched with a mastery of marketing and modern business methods. Every seat in the Million Dollar Theatre had a switch that activated when someone sat down, lighting up a house diagram so the usherettes could direct patrons to empty seats and Grauman could maintain a close eye on attendance.

He opened two more theaters nearby, the Rialto and the Metropolitan, before sussing out that Hollywood was destined to be the city's entertainment district. So Grauman unloaded all three to refocus in the new hot spot. First came his Egyptian Theater, capitalizing on the buzz generated by the 1922 discovery of King Tut's tomb. A few years later, he opened the Chinese Theater across the street. Each was built to accommodate even more extravagant

Edison Building, Los Angeles – 1918
307 South Broadway

prologues and premieres. But the advent of sound pictures sapped audience enthusiasm for the old fashioned way of going to the movies. Studio heads began to limit showings of their first-run films to screens they owned, creating more challenges for an independent operator like Grauman, who had an extensive payroll to meet for his singers, dancers, and musicians. By the early 1930s, he was out of show business.

Grauman never married, and there are rumors that he was gay, even that he hosted flamboyant private parties at the Million Dollar Theatre in the days before gay bars were tolerated. After his death, a Texas waitress tried to claim part of his estate, saying she had been Grauman's common-law wife for four years in California. The case was dismissed after a handwriting expert concluded the plaintiff had forged a purported "will" the famous showman was alleged to have scrawled in blue crayon. Grauman, had he been in the courtroom, might have found it amusing. He was famous for pranks—both giving and receiving them. When Warner Brothers opened a competing theater on Hollywood Boulevard, he arrived at its opening in a hearse and had pallbearers carry him into the gala in a coffin. Silver screen star Myrna Loy, who got her break as a Grauman chorus girl, showed up for her cement footprint ceremony in floppy clown shoes.

With Grauman gone, the Million Dollar Theatre eventually enjoyed a midcentury renaissance as a Spanish-language movie house. Today it occasionally holds screenings of classic films, providing a rare opportunity to appreciate its spectacular auditorium. The fantastical exterior and archways that explode with helmeted cherubs and bison is not what one would expect for the headquarters of an electric company. Nor does it seem suited for another noteworthy former tenant, water department chief engineer William Mulholland, designer of the Los Angeles Aqueduct and namesake of the city's famous drive. Cinema buffs who visit should not leave without first crossing the street to see the Bradbury Building, whose birdcage of wrought iron staircases and banisters have served as a memorable film set in pictures as varied as "(500) Days of Summer," "The Artist," and "Blade Runner."

LUHRS BUILDING — Phoenix

"Lighthouse of Phoenix Prosperity" read one hyperbolic news headline when Arizona debuted its first skyscraper. A classical cornice, balconies, and large arched windows add undeniable panache to what would otherwise be an unexceptional ten-story office block. But the Luhrs Building's owner knew how far Phoenix had come, and how fast—he boasted that his parents owned the first bathtub in town.

At the age of twenty, Georg Luhrs left Germany in 1867 and went to California, first working as a wheelwright, a trade he learned from his father. He tried prospecting in Nevada. Though he had no success striking it rich, Luhrs got a job as a foreman of wagonmakers for a gold mine in Wickenburg, Arizona. It was a dangerous place, and not only in the mineshaft. The superintendent's son was ambushed by a Yavapai raiding party, and his corpse was found the next day with forty arrows in it.

Luhrs moved in 1878 to Phoenix, which began as a farming community to supply Wickenburg. He and a blacksmith ran a wagonmaking and repair shop with a stable and corral. Georg played accordion at town dances and was elected to city council in 1883. The following year, during a visit to his old hometown, he courted the girl next door, Gretchen. They married and returned to a house in Phoenix, where Gretchen gave birth to a son and two daughters. By the end of the decade, they also were owners and managers of a three-story hotel, where their youngest son, George Jr., was born.

When the boy was six, William McKinley came to town, so they dressed their son up as Uncle Sam. The amused commander-in-chief let the lad sit on his lap. George seemed fond of costumes; he held onto his grade school band uniform the rest of his life. He especially loved music. He gave schoolmates private violin lessons in high school, and was an accomplished young tenor, winning a state singing contest his senior year.

George Jr. never dated and never married, explaining in his memoirs that he was too busy for the ladies. He does mention two women he fancied, though both stories are rather chaste: one was his co-star in the high school musical, the other was a childhood friend he caught up with in college and would

Luhrs Building, Phoenix – 1924
11 West Jefferson Street

visit at her family's home to sing while she accompanied him on piano. In the end, he spent most of his adult years living in the hotel with his widowed sister, sharing the same bedroom.

On the other hand, George Jr. spends considerably more time in the memoirs describing his male friends from college. One, he coyly notes, sent him "very interesting letters" from abroad. There was Myron, a fellow glee club member from Stanford five years George Jr.'s junior. Myron played piano at a mountain resort, and George Jr. spent a week with him there on several occasions. The pair also took a coast-to-coast train tour together in the summer of 1921, after George Jr. got his law degree. They looped from New Orleans to New York, then Montreal, Chicago, and Vancouver before returning to California for Myron's senior year of college, where the young men "found it both hard to part." George Jr. also describes entertaining his fellow masons at a San Francisco convention by performing mock native dances for them in a hotel lobby "wearing nothing but a G-string."

While his older brother ran the hotel, the office tower was primarily George Jr.'s doing. It was dedicated to his mother and father—their names were on the cornerstone—and they watched it rise from their hotel across the street. He worked out the financing and secured the tenants, starting with the private Arizona Club, which took the top four floors. In addition to banquets and balls—one barnyard-themed dance had haystacks and chickens in the lobby—the businessmen's club sometimes hosted prizefights on the roof.

Five years later, George Jr. built another office building, the slightly taller Art Deco Luhrs Tower, on the other side of the block. At one time the complex housed both the state Prohibition headquarters and a front company for mob-controlled bookmakers. The latter was run by mobster Gus Greenbaum, who would go on to manage two Las Vegas hotels before getting whacked along with his wife in their Phoenix home in 1958. Nowadays, the building where federal agents used to dump confiscated booze down the cellar drain is home to a stylish cocktail bar.

7

International

L ike most of the people who built them or rode their elevators to work every day, the first skyscrapers were born in America of European lineage. Their designers stood on the shoulders of Old World engineers and architects. They studied in Paris and took their inspiration from towering Gothic cathedrals, Greek temples, and bell towers from Renaissance Italy and Spain.

Europe's influence did not come solely from the past. The Eiffel Tower was a feat of engineering contemporaneous with America's first skyscrapers and a profound statement that the continent was capable of producing structures of tremendous height and grace. But another European far less famous than Gustave Eiffel probably contributed more to the art of tall buildings.

The Oriel Chambers by Peter Ellis on Liverpool's main thoroughfare is interesting enough to draw an appreciative glance from the occasional passerby today. But when it first opened in 1864, the five-story block shocked onlookers. Instead of brick or stone walls filling in the spaces between its cast iron framework, the Oriel Chambers had plate glass. Large projecting windows—called oriel windows, hence the name—were arrayed side-by-side and stacked three floors high on both of the building's street-facing sides.

More window than stone: the 1864 Oriel Chambers in Liverpool

It was enough to make the traditionalists shriek. The British architectural journal *The Builder* savaged the Oriel Chambers, calling it "a sight to make the angels weep" and further stating:

> *The plainest brick warehouse in the town is infinitely superior, as a building, to that large agglomeration of protruding plate-glass bubbles in Water Street, termed Oriel Chambers. Did we not see this vast abortion—which would be depressing were it not ludicrous—with our own eyes, we should have doubted the possibility of its existence.*

The Civil War was raging in America when the Oriel Chambers opened. That year, a nervous father in Atlanta put his fourteen-year-old son on a blockade runner bound for Liverpool, hoping to save the boy from possible conscription. The first letter home from young John Root raved that "the streets are lined with handsome buildings." Already interested in architecture, the boy waited out the war as a student in Liverpool, then returned to study engineering in college in New York. Two years after graduating, he moved to Chicago, where he met Daniel Burnham. Their partnership set the vocabulary of skyscrapers—including projecting ranks of bay windows pioneered by an obscure British architect.

Few European cities had any skyscrapers, even as they were filling American skylines. When authorities in Rome bounced around the idea of putting a supertall tower in the city center, the newspaper *La Tribuna* objected: "The building also reminds us of New York City's infamous skyscrapers, and we doubt that our city will be a suitable environment for it."

But Europeans remained in the vanguard of ideas for skyscrapers, even if most of their countrymen didn't like them. The international contest to design the Tribune Tower in Chicago elicited a number of noteworthy entries from continental architects. The much-heralded second prize winner by Eliel Saarinen of Finland became a template for the Art Deco style. German entrant Walter Gropius, founder of the Bauhaus school, presented the judges with a boxy glass-and-steel concept completely devoid of ornamentation. The style became known as International, and skyscrapers of that type proliferated in cities around the world.

Yet America maintained its lead through the twentieth century as the undisputed champion of skyscrapers, the country with the biggest and best. That lasted until 1998, when the concrete Petronas Towers in Kuala Lumpur took world's tallest honors from the Sears Tower after its thirty years in the pole position. Unless they didn't.

Proud Chicagoans protested—not without justification—that the top floor and roof of the Sears Tower were both considerably farther off the ground than the corresponding bits of the Malaysian structure. Its spires added an extra 240 feet to the Petronas, whereas the even taller antennas atop the Chicago skyscraper were not considered to be structurally integral, and therefore did not count towards its architectural height.

Taiwan next joined the fray, with a skyscraper whose top floor slightly edged the Sears but whose spire still did not quite reach the apex of the Sears antenna. The Burj Khalifa settled the question, blasting several hundred feet beyond the others by any conceivable measurement. Almost as though signaling defeat, the Chicago building's owners sold the naming rights to a British insurance company in 2009 as the Dubai tower neared completion. Its new designation of Willis Tower has enjoyed less than wholehearted public acceptance.

As of this writing, of the twenty tallest skyscrapers in the world, the United States claims two. Both are in Manhattan: One World Trade Center—its spire counts—and the brand new Central Park Tower.

China has ten. It also has six more under construction that will be tall enough to make the list when they are finished in the next few years.

* * *

Witte Huis, Rotterdam – 1898
Geldersekade 1

WITTE HUIS — Rotterdam

Despite its name meaning White House, Europe's first skyscraper completely looks its continental part. A colorful fairytale castle with striped awnings over its windows and a steeply pitched roof, the turreted tower eleven stories tall stands amid quaint canals and rows of parked bicycles. Its original owners hailed from a Rotterdam shipping family, and the idea for their building was sparked by a voyage to another major seaport at the mouth of a great river—the one Dutch traders formerly knew as New Amsterdam.

The Witte Huis (pronounced "*WIT-tuh hous*") was built for the brothers Gerrit and Herman van der Schuijt, whose father was a shipbuilder and engine manufacturer. The two were only a few years out of school in 1885 when they went into business with a factory making industrial lubricants. Ten years later, Gerrit, the older of the two, sailed to New York with another brother who was on leave from his job as a technician for Royal Dutch Petroleum in Sumatra. They may have visited a relative of theirs in Brooklyn who was also in the oil business. What is certain is that Gerrit was beguiled by the skyscrapers he saw in Manhattan, particularly a tall luxury hotel at the southeast corner of Central Park called the New Netherlands Hotel.

Back home in Rotterdam, Gerrit and Herman bought land in the old harbor near the Meuse River, at the landing spot of a large new bridge named for the recently deceased King Willem III. They hired a local architect, Willem Molenbroek, to build them a house in town and also draw up an office building for their harbor parcel. Its design resembles a junior version of the New Netherland, with turrets, gables, and a steep mansard roof like the New York building. But instead of the rough stone Richardsonian Romanesque look popular in the United States, Molenbroek went with the European turn-of-the-century style known as Art Nouveau. His Witte Huis has a two-story stone base carved with flower and dragon motifs, topped by a white glazed brick facade accented with patterns of yellow, blue, and red bricks.

Skeptics said Rotterdam's soil was too marshy for such a heavy structure, and indeed during excavation a neighboring building collapsed. The van der Schuijts simply bought that property and added it to the Witte Huis footprint. The building is supported by nine hundred pilings that extend fifty feet down. After its opening in 1898, the owners were able to lease the offices at satisfactory rates, earning enough to cover building expenses and pay dividends to bondholders. They had no such success with their next venture, purchasing one hundred fifty acres of riverside land in south Rotterdam with the intention of developing a neighborhood. Delays in that project and shifting land value left them insolvent, and in 1903 the brothers and their architect declared bankruptcy. All three had to vacate their seventh-floor offices in the Witte Huis. Gerrit moved to Paris, and Herman sailed for the Dutch East Indies.

Because of its strategic location overlooking a key bridge, the Witte Huis played a central role in the Dutch army's desperate but ultimately futile resistance against the Nazi onslaught of 1940. In one of the first engagements of the invasion, German paratroopers seized the bridge and set up a beachhead in an office building on the north bank of the river. About a football field away, Dutch soldiers mounted machine guns in the upper floors of the Witte Huis. They waged a ferocious battle for three days, neither side able to expel the other. Then the Luftwaffe squadrons arrived to bomb Rotterdam—and the Netherlands—into submission. Most of the city was destroyed, and the Dutch surrendered. But miraculously, the Witte Huis remained standing.

Bullet holes that once pockmarked the facade were filled in long ago, but not all the damage was repaired. The building once had six life-size statues standing in niches along the second floor. The allegorical figures for Shipping, Progress, Agriculture, Industry, and Trade are still there, but one niche is empty after the sixth statue, Labor, was destroyed in the fighting and never replaced.

The observatory level on top of the three-story iron roof offers an excellent vantage point to appreciate Rotterdam's skyline of modern and postmodern construction. It didn't happen as rapidly as the van der Schuijts might have liked, but their hometown became a skyscraper city after all.

ROYAL LIVER BUILDING — Liverpool

This imposing concrete and granite pile standing like a shore battery at the head of the Mersey River pier is as much a symbol of Liverpool as the two bird statues perched like sentinels on its crest. It was the tallest skyscraper in Europe for nearly thirty years, starting with the coronation of a king and ending the year of the Luftwaffe raids. But the bombs did not end its reign; a taller Italian building did that.

The clock, called Great George, is Britain's largest at twenty-five feet in diameter—two feet bigger than Big Ben's timepiece in Westminster. Controlled by a signal from Greenwich observatory, its electronic ticker was turned on to much fanfare on June 22, 1911, as George V was being crowned in Westminster Abbey. The building stands on reclaimed land that once was George's Dock. That name honored an earlier monarch in 1771, when the dock first offered its berths to the spice-hauling schooners and slave ships that made Liverpool into a wealthy port.

For those who did not share in the city's prosperity, death could be an especially dreadful prospect. Without savings, one could be dumped into a common paupers grave, leaving behind a destitute widow and children. That was the problem John Lawrence was discussing with his friends one night in 1850 down at their pub, the Royal Lyver (this and Liver without the -pool both rhyme with "striver," not "river"). Lawrence, a former sailor, had started working for a mutual aid group and proposed they should start their own. With eight other people, Lawrence founded the Royal Liver Friendly Society that year, with the main office in his home. Members made regular payments to a fund that promised to cover expenses for burial with dignity in a private grave. So many people joined that the organization hired two professional outsiders to manage its rapid growth, and they soon dispensed with Lawrence.

As the fund ballooned over the years, so did the remuneration of the two senior managers. That lasted until Edward Taunton, the chief clerk at the head office, raised an alarm about the executives getting unreasonably rich off the organization's working class policyholders. A government inquiry followed, and Taunton advocated reforms that included bouncing the two greedy executives and shifting control to a board of delegates made up of those insured by the society. It held its first annual meeting in 1887, with Taunton as secretary. A week later, illness took him at the age of thirty-seven. Taunton's brother, Frank, succeeded him and served as secretary for the next thirty years.

The society voted in 1907 to buy a parcel in the newly-filled former George's Dock and build a skyscraper. They chose a local architect, Aubrey Thomas, who had just designed a steel-framed office block across the street from the site in question. The cornerstone was laid in 1908 by Lord Edward Stanley of Alderley. A senior trustee of the society and proponent of public education reforms, he was the younger brother and successor of Lord Henry Stanley, a world traveler who converted to Islam and was the first Muslim member of the House of Lords.

The statues on the roof portray a mythical creature, the liver bird, that has been the city emblem for centuries and is featured on the badge of Liverpool Football Club. It is believed to have originated in 1207, when King John first chartered Liverpool as a town. The story goes that an artist was told to make a town seal featuring the royal heraldic eagle. As he had never seen one, his design turned out closer to a cormorant, a seabird prevalent in the northwest of England. The artist responsible for the eighteen-foot copper roof sculptures was a German-born woodcarver, Carl Bartels, who had brought his bride to Britain for their honeymoon in 1887 and decided to stay. Despite being a naturalized British citizen and the creator of Liverpool's most iconic public art, Bartels was arrested during World War I, along with thousands of other native Germans, after a furor erupted when a U-boat sank the Lusitania on its way to Liverpool. He spent three years in an internment camp separated from his wife and children, and at war's end was forcibly repatriated to Germany. Bartels ultimately won permission to return, but was not recognized again for the birds until long after his death.

When the two countries went to war for the second time, Liverpool was Britain's most bombed target outside London. Nearly two thousand residents were killed in the Blitz, and seventy thousand lost their homes. The docks

Royal Liver Building, Liverpool – 1911
Pier Head

were the main target, and half the berths were knocked out of commission. But the Royal Liver Building weathered the destruction nearly unscathed. It suffered rocket damage eighty years later, when a rowdy teenager celebrating Liverpool's first English soccer title in three decades shot a firework at the building and started a minor blaze.

A London mutual insurance group acquired Royal Liver in 2011, and one of the last votes by the society delegates was to put their building up for sale. It was purchased by a Luxembourg investment group five years later, and locals gasped when it was discovered that one of the partners was the owner of the city's other soccer club, Everton. The building has been thoroughly modernized on the inside, though traces of the marble paneling remain. In 2019 an attraction opened that for the first time allows the public to climb up inside Great George and onto the tower above it. There can be no better vantage point to watch ferries cross the Mersey.

WORLD BUILDING — Vancouver

This Vancouver landmark only kept its original name for a decade, but the man responsible for it had much more staying power. Louis Taylor holds the record for longest serving mayor in the city's history. Mostly he did it the hard way, one-year term by one-year term, running sixteen mayoral campaigns and losing half of them.

Vancouver's winningest—and losingest—mayor was an American immigrant from Ann Arbor, Michigan. He and a partner operated a private bank in Chicago beginning in 1896. But the partner took off for Mexico, leaving the bank insolvent. Taylor spent a night in jail facing charges of embezzlement, and after making bail, he hopped a train for Vancouver, leaving his wife and infant son behind. There he worked as a railroad baggage handler and made a couple abortive efforts to strike it rich prospecting for gold.

After Taylor became a Canadian citizen in 1900, he sent for his wife and boy. They did not stay long, but relocated to Los Angeles to live with her parents. At about the same time, he got a job at a struggling Vancouver newspaper as circulation manager. That went well, so he decided to raise his visibility for a career in politics by pooling together investors and buying the city's Liberal party organ, the *Vancouver World*. One investor put up the money on the condition that Taylor find a job for his widowed daughter, Alice Berry. She became business manager, and the two became amorous.

Taylor improved the *World*'s coverage and grew its circulation—partly with racist anti-immigrant harangues. Exhorting members of the city's Asiatic Exclusion League to "preserve British Columbia for white people," Taylor ran for the group's presidency but lost. The next year, in 1909, he ran for Vancouver mayor and lost. But he was back again battling in the following year's election, and this time he won. He was reelected after pushing through an eight-hour workday for city employees and persuading council to limit real estate taxes to the land only, not buildings or improvements, so as to promote growth. "A new skyline is being built up for the city, a skyline of tall, substantial buildings of stone and granite," Taylor said.

He was speaking from experience. In 1909 he had formed a company to erect a skyscraper for his newspaper. When it opened three years later, the tower topped out at seventeen stories, passing the nearby Dominion Building as Canada's tallest offices. Some commented that nine topless muses along the roofline hinted at the mayor's live-and-let-live views on vice—while prostitution was illegal, the brothels in Chinatown and other poor districts were mostly left alone provided they kept policemen's palms greased.

Unfortunately for Taylor, he lost the election the year his skyscraper opened—and the year after that, and the year after that, too. The third loss, in 1914, was the lowlight of a dismal year, as his paper faced increasing competition and reduced ad revenues while its underoccupied office building lacked sufficient lease revenue to cover costs. In 1915 Taylor managed to win back the mayoralty, but he had little time to celebrate. The day after the election, he was in court, ordered to sell the newspaper and the building to pay off creditors. The building's new owner was the publisher of the rival *Vancouver Sun*, which is why it has been known as Sun Tower ever since.

Taylor eventually divorced his wife and married Alice, and the two started up a small magazine. Their wedded bliss lasted three years until Alice died of a blood disorder. Alone again, Taylor decided to give politics another go. Now in his mid-sixties, he lost another three straight elections before winning again in 1925, despite this editorial comment from his old newspaper: "A vote for Taylor is a reckless plunge into the dark."

It almost ended in grisly fashion. At a ceremony inaugurating passenger service from Seattle to Victoria in 1928, Taylor disembarked from the maiden flight and walked directly under a spinning propeller. Luckily he was short, so it only split his skull rather than decapitating him. More elections followed—a few wins, a few more losses—until well-wishers finally set up a trust and begged him to retire. After his death, the city renamed a home for indigent elderly in his honor.

The tower recently has undergone extensive restoration work, including a costly upgrade to the domed roof. It was once covered with tiles painted a green patina to suggest a copper roof exposed to the elements. The current owners have replaced the tiles with real copper plates.

World Building, Vancouver – 1912
128 West Pender Street

Palacio Barolo, Buenos Aires – 1923
Avenida de Mayo 1370

PALACIO BAROLO — Buenos Aires

Argentina's capital is often described as a South American mixture of Madrid, Paris, and Barcelona because of its blend of continental architectural styles. But this skyscraper a few blocks from the national parliament defies simple categorization—if anything, it seems to come from the Star Wars planet of Naboo. It was designed by an Italian architect for an Italian businessman who wanted to use the building as a tomb for the major Italian poet Dante Alighieri. When that plan failed to materialize, the architect burned out his career in a futile struggle to build the world's biggest skyscraper for another larger-than-life Italian, Benito Mussolini.

Luis Barolo was part of the wave of Italian immigrants who came to Argentina in the late nineteenth century. Arriving in 1890 as a young man from the Piedmont, Barolo built a successful textile business in Argentina spinning cotton and wool with imported machines. Separated by an ocean, he grew increasingly anxious about the fate of his native land, especially after Italy lost half a million soldiers in World War I. When he was wealthy enough to build a high-rise in his adopted home, Barolo wanted it to play a role in preserving western civilization. In the middle of the lobby, he would have a sarcophagus built for Dante's mortal remains, which for centuries had been entombed at Ravenna. The skyscraper sepulchre would open in 1921, in time for the six hundredth anniversary of the poet's passing.

For his architect, Barolo chose a fellow Italian with a similar eye for the grandiloquent gesture. Mario Palanti had studied in Milan before coming to Buenos Aires with a classmate to oversee construction of their teacher's project, an Italian pavilion for Argentina's 1910 centennial exposition. Both young men stuck around to open their own private practices; the classmate, Francisco Gianotti, designed Galería Güemes, the city's first skyscraper, and the café El Molino, both brilliant examples of the Art Nouveau style. Palanti returned to Italy in 1915 to volunteer as a military engineer during the war. Upon his return to Buenos Aires, he put on an exhibition of drawings of monumental architecture, such as a mountaintop temple dedicated to universal peace.

Barolo found a kindred spirit in Palanti, whose plans for his building were a complex homage to Dante's *Divine Comedy*, both in terms of its allegorical subject matter and its underlying numerology. It comprises three parts tracking the progress of Dante's poetic journey from the infernal to the divine: lower floors represent hell, the middle floors are purgatory, and the tower and lighthouse are paradise. Its height of one hundred meters matches the number of cantos in the poet's masterwork, and the rows of eleven windows across the front represent the eleven syllables in every one of its lines of verse. Unfortunately, the building was not ready in 1921 for Dante's bones, even if authorities in Italy could have been persuaded to part with them. The namesake of the Palacio Barolo died frustrated before its opening in 1923.

But the tallest skyscraper in South America was an eye-catcher. Its style was neither classical nor renaissance nor Art Nouveau, but an eclecticism that was purely Palanti's. He modeled the dome, for instance, after an eleventh-century Indian temple. The Salvo brothers, another Italian family in the South American textile business, asked him to design a similar tower for them in Montevideo, Uruguay, across the Río de la Plata. Slightly taller, it contains no Dante references but does share the somewhat bulbous forms of the Palacio Barolo, and it also has a lighthouse on its roof. (When the Palacio Salvo opened in 1928, Le Corbusier, the Swiss architect and sworn enemy of decorations, called it "a monstrous copulation of American and Italian pastry.")

With two unique skyscrapers under his belt, Palanti went for the gusto. He proposed an unprecedentedly huge skyscraper in 1924 for the new regime in Rome. It would be eighty-eight stories, taller than anything including the Eiffel Tower, and house not only offices but assembly and concert halls, sports facilities, and the Italian national legislature—plus a lighthouse on top. He called it L'Eternale, and sent details to Italy's charismatic Fascist prime minister, Benito Mussolini. Mussolini sent Palanti a signed photo, and the architect went to Rome to put on an exhibition of his L'Eternale drawings. He also brought an Argentine greyhound as a gift for Mussolini, who signed the exhibit guest book with the Fascist cheer of "Alalà!"

Initial press reports treated it as a done deal, but critics began to question the wisdom of plopping such a monolith in the middle of the Eternal City. Cass Gilbert, whose Woolworth Building stood to lose its designation of world's tallest skyscraper, wrote Il Duce an obsequious letter suggesting he reconsider. Eventually Mussolini cooled on L'Eternale. But Palanti refused to give up. In 1932 he entered another competition to design a great Fascist party headquarters. He even left his new wife in the middle of a beach holiday to catch a boat to Rome, hoping to curry favor with Mussolini by presenting him with another animal—this time a stallion. Unfortunately for Palanti, not only did he fail to win over the Italian dictator, but his soon-to-be ex-wife went ballistic when she learned he had tried to give away her horse without so much as asking permission. Palanti stayed in Italy after their divorce teaching architecture, but only built one building there the rest of his life: the family tomb, where he was laid to rest in 1978.

Tours are given daily at the Palacio Barolo. Guides can elaborate in Spanish and English upon the many references to Dante, and to Italy in general, such as the color scheme of red, white, and green and the Latin quotes inscribed on the vaulted ceilings. The lobby is part of the inferno section of the building, so the sculptures are of serpents and other scary creatures. Brass grills on the floor lit from below represent the fires of hell. Visitors rub the head of a sculpted bronze South American condor shown carrying Dante's body to the heavens; it is a copy of a much larger original that was meant to adorn the poet's sarcophagus but was stolen before the building was complete. Those willing to climb the tower's narrow stairs are rewarded with a panoramic view.

Even at that height, it is too far to see the light from the Palacio Barolo's twin building in Montevideo, one hundred miles across the water. But those who make the trip will discover a tango museum at the Palacio Salvo. The tower stands on the former site of the café where "La Cumparsita," the ur-tango, was first performed. This annoys Argentines, who zealously guard their patrimony of the genre, but a Uruguayan student named Hernán Matos Rodríguez composed the most famous tango. The teenager preferred songwriting to the boring textbooks in his course of study—architecture.

Royal Bank Tower, Montreal - 1928
360 Rue Saint-Jacques

ROYAL BANK TOWER — Montreal

Is it worth the trouble and expense to have the biggest skyscraper in the land? When the board of directors of Canada's largest bank were faced with this question, they answered with a resounding yes—not just once, but three times. The Royal Bank of Canada cut the ribbon on the country's tallest office building in 1915, 1928, and 1962.

The institution was founded in Halifax, Nova Scotia, by merchants desiring to facilitate trade of cargo arriving at the wharves. As it grew, it relocated to Montreal, adopted the name Royal Bank of Canada, and started opening branches across the country. After the founding president, a Halifax dry goods merchant named Thomas Kenny, died in 1908, his replacement was an Irish immigrant who had ascended to a place among Montreal's business elite.

Herbert Holt studied engineering at Trinity College in Dublin before coming to Canada. His first job was in Ontario, assisting with the construction of two railroad lines near Toronto. Then his boss, James Ross, was hired as the construction manager for the Canadian Pacific Railroad as the project undertook its push over the Rocky Mountains to the Pacific coast. Ross brought along Holt as his superintendent. When that considerable task was completed, they continued as partners for further railroad ventures on the Canadian prairie before eventually switching focus to developing electric streetcars in Montreal. When Royal Bank of Canada came calling, Holt was also president of Montreal Light, Heat and Power. And he was just getting started—Holt ultimately claimed to have served on three hundred corporate boards.

Under his direction and that of Edson Pease, the bank's managing director and CEO, the Royal Bank of Canada adopted a strategy of growth by merger. The bank swallowed up several smaller financial institutions to extend its reach across the provinces; it simultaneously expanded its operations into Cuba and throughout the Caribbean. Called before a House of Commons finance committee to explain his institution's aggressive moves, Holt said mergers put banking in Canada on a sound footing by removing weak and unstable institutions. "In union there is strength," he explained.

In 1915, Royal Bank of Canada opened its first skyscraper, a twenty-story Beaux-Arts tower in Toronto's financial district that took the crown of Canada's tallest office from Vancouver's World Building. Twelve years later, Holt laid the cornerstone for the building that supplanted it. The Royal Bank of Canada headquarters at 360 Rue Saint-Jacques in Montreal was the tallest structure not only in Canada, but in the entire British Commonwealth, edging past the Royal Liver Building. Inside, it took the concept of the resplendent banking lobby to new heights, with forty-five-foot vaulted ceilings soaring above travertine floors. Montreal zoning rules required most of the building's twenty-two stories to be recessed from the property line. They permitted its monumental four-story base, with arched windows topped by a two-story colonnade, to kiss up against the sidewalk.

Not one to let his bank responsibilities get in the way of his corporate interests, Holt parlayed his experience arranging bank mergers, consolidating Canadian firms in the pulp and paper industries and in steel production, expanding his personal influence. He also began relying on his bank to make loans to his various business ventures, a situation that eventually led to problems. When the pulp and paper business slumped and could not meet debt payments, the bank began an internal investigation into questionable loans.

The Great Depression squeezed credit lines even tighter. So when the president of the Montreal stock exchange, a broker named W.E.J. Luther, came to Holt in 1932 to request the Royal Bank's assistance in keeping his firm out of bankruptcy, Holt declined. With that, the desperate man pulled out a pistol and shot the seventy-six-year-old bank president, who dived under his desk. Assuming he had killed Holt, Luther sped home and committed suicide in his garage by carbon monoxide poisoning. But Holt lived, though he used his influence to ensure that no news of his shooting ever got into the papers. He retired a couple years later, accepted the sinecure of chairman, and departed to warmer climes to enjoy his mansion in the Bahamas.

Decades later, Royal Bank of Canada again relocated to the tallest skyscraper in Canada. This time it was Place Ville-Marie, a forty-seven-story International style steel and glass box by I.M. Pei. The bank continued to operate its branch in the 1928 tower until 2010, when it left for good. Fortunately, the great banking hall was beautifully preserved and is used now for rentable co-working spaces and conference rooms. It also has a public café, making it Montreal's most elegant place to enjoy a cappuccino and bagel.

Epilogue

Poor Henry James. Skyscrapers ruined his childhood memories.

The celebrated novelist grew up in New York City in the years before the Civil War, the second of four boys in a well-to-do family living on a bountiful inheritance. James was twelve when his parents took him and his brothers to Europe. They spent a full five years there, moving around from France to England to Switzerland before coming home. He went back several times as he got older, and eventually settled in London. He wrote *The Portrait of a Lady* there, and *The Wings of A Dove*, and many other acclaimed works. The life of American emigres in Europe became his signature theme.

When he came back to New York in 1904 for the first time in twenty-one years, James did not like what he found. *The American Scene*, a book he wrote after a year of traveling throughout his native country, is shot through with pessimism. Among the many things that stuck in his craw were skyscrapers.

It made him feel old, James wrote, to see "the new landmarks crushing the old quite as violent children stamp on snails and caterpillars." The house where he was born had been replaced with a "high, square, impersonal structure," he harrumphed. Worse, nobody had bothered to place a historical marker or plaque there to indicate it was the birthplace of a famous author. Such plaques were quite often found in Europe, James noted with approval, but such a thing was "unthinkable" in skyscraper-mad New York. Where would one even put it?

In James's view, the motive of New York's powerful developers was crystal clear. They preferred tall buildings because the public could never warm to them like they did with older buildings. They would be easy to replace when the owners tired of them. Skyscrapers, he said, reeked of "insincerity." One that came in for special vitriol was the Trinity Building, a twenty-one-story tower next to the city's landmark church. It was, according to James, like a mountain threatening to bury Trinity Church in an avalanche.

Yet in his diatribe, James conveniently omitted several key details. First, the new tower hadn't encroached on the church; it replaced another large office building, a five-story block that had stood there since 1853. If he thought back, James had surely seen it as a kid growing up in Manhattan. The earlier building had been designed by Richard Upjohn, the architect of Trinity Church. Upjohn and several other architects kept offices in the building, which enjoyed a prime business address near the intersection of Wall Street and Broadway.

Second, that building had replaced another structure that dated back to 1754. That one had been six stories tall, though its floors were smaller than the typical office height because it was not an office. It was a warehouse for storing and refining sugarcane from the West Indies, and it had an infamous history. During the Revolutionary War, while the British occupied New York City, they used that sugar house and others in the city as prisons for their American captives. The sugar house that stood next to the churchyard was notorious for a sadistic sergeant who ran it. Up to four hundred prisoners at a time crammed inside its windowless walls in the filthy gloom, prey to outbreaks of smallpox and cholera, surviving on moldy starvation rations, and subject to beatings from the guards for the merest infraction, such as requesting pen and paper to write to their wives and families.

Third, there was a plaque. Even nicer than the ones in Europe that James was so fond of. It had been put there in 1852, when the old sugar house was torn down to build the offices for architects. The stone tablet, and the tall memorial Gothic spire it was attached to, were just a few steps from the sidewalk where James worked up his fury over the skyscraper. It was dedicated "to the Memory of those great and good Men who died whilst in Captivity in the old Sugar House and were interred in Trinity Church Yard in this City."

It is still there today. So is the Trinity Building. So is Trinity Church.

* * *

Other people liked skyscrapers. One such person was Katharine Lee Bates, who taught English literature at Wellesley College. In 1893, she got a summer job lecturing in the spa town of Colorado Springs. On the way there, Bates stopped in Chicago to connect with her girlfriend, another Wellesley professor, and the two of them visited the World's Fair. They were overwhelmed by the dazzling White City, and made plans to come back when the summer was over. Then they got on a train and headed west.

One day when class was not in session, Bates joined an excursion to the summit of Pikes Peak. The climbers rode in a wagon, then transferred to mules for the broken, rocky trail above the tree line. As Bates took in the scene, the words of a poem suddenly came to her—something about purple mountains above the fruited plain.

She wrote the whole thing down that night, all four stanzas. Then she put it away and went back to the women's college outside Boston. She and the other professor, Katharine Coman, moved in together and lived as a couple from then on. Eventually Bates took out the poem again, made a few minor revisions, and offered it for publication. The rest is history.

She kept her original lines in the last stanza. Not the one about dramatic landscapes, or pilgrim feet, or liberating strife. The one that imagines the magnificent cities of the future. A hymn of skyscrapers.

O beautiful for patriot dream
That sees beyond the years
Thine alabaster cities gleam
Undimmed by human tears.
America! America!
God shed His grace on thee,
And crown thy good with brotherhood
From sea to shining sea.

Trinity Church and the Trinity Building on Broadway in New York.
The memorial spire to American soldiers who died imprisoned at the sugar house
is in the churchyard by the large tree.

Acknowledgements

Writing a book during the annus horribilis of 2020 makes the concept of gratitude even more poignant. I must start by thanking Brian Hyslop, who helped me to create the monthly column that was the first iteration of MultiStories for *Pittsburgh Magazine*, and Cindi Lash, who first invited me to write about antique skyscrapers for those pages. Both editors offered bountiful encouragement and invaluable advice.

I also am grateful to Karamagi Rujumba and Arthur Ziegler of Pittsburgh History and Landmarks Foundation for launching my public speaking career on this topic, and to Bonnie Baxter of Doors Open Pittsburgh for helping me plan and offer antique skyscraper rooftop tours. I owe Jeff Tobe sincere thanks for supplying the impetus for this book and for sticking around to offer essential guidance in the planning stages. Jonathan Potts gets my deep appreciation for being a great boss and supporting my writing. For their professional feedback and support, I am especially thankful to Rick Sebak, Peg Breen, Alan Axelrod, Jim Hunt, and Donovan Rypkema.

Visiting so many cities over a two-year period is a tall order under any circumstances, especially with pandemic travel restrictions. I'm grateful to the following people who helped me to personally visit 47 of the 55 antique skyscrapers: Vincent Bertrand, Christine Chiarello, Tilly Clark, Helen Post Curry, Amber Davis, Sarah Gilliam, Mark Goins, Jano Nixon Kelley, Mike Kless, Avery Leslie, Jim MacIlvaine, Cole Mansfield, Michelle McCoy, Andrew Milke, Jim Owczarski, Matt Rinker, Eric Rogers, Marie Rowley, Louis Rucker, Jodi Sokup, Wanda Texon, Kim Thornton, Joleen Zanuzoski, and Brennan Zerbe. I appreciated the research assistance of Douglas DeCroix at Western New York Heritage, Ashlie Hand at the Diocese of Kansas City-St. Joseph, Traci Patterson at Rice University, Susan Reynolds at the University of Alabama,

Louis Rucker at the Wainwright State Office Building, and Rebecca Smith at the Historic New Orleans Collection.

Special thanks to Cole Mansfield at the Staypineapple Chicago, Bill Bacelieri at the Hotel Indigo Nashville, and Melody Lanthorn at the Pioneer Square Courtyard by Marriott in Seattle (also known as the Alaska Building, the best antique skyscraper to narrowly miss inclusion in this book) for showing me their beautiful properties and arranging for me to stay in them overnight. Extra special thanks to Emily Anderson for taking an excellent author photo atop the Niels Esperson Building, to Dan Driscoll for a breathtaking tour of the World Building scaffolding and for an original roof tile I somehow got through airport security, to Megan Filarski for a couple of comped cocktails that made the Smith Tower even more stupendous, and Larry Walsh for showing me Henry Clay Frick's personal office and Jules Verne–style shower massage nozzles.

A writer is lucky to have the support of a close friend who knows from experience what it takes to write a book. I have two. Gary Sizer honored me by letting me edit his hilarious travel tales, and in doing so gave me several lessons in the amount of work involved. Andrew Conte has helped me to grow as a writer going all the way back to our newspaper days, and was essential in converting me from a skeptic to an author. I am indebted to both for their feedback and support, and for making life more delightful through their friendship.

My children have inspired me all their lives. If there is one good thing about the pandemic, it is that it put them all back in my house to appreciate again what blessings God has given me. It filled me with pride to see Cricket put together such a brilliant cover design, and Rachael with her careful proofreading helped soothe my writer's paranoia. Tessa and Theodore both showed me by example how to cope with life's unexpected obstacles, which gave me strength to roll with each uncertainty that arose.

Behind the scenes and through it all, my lovely and loving wife, Diane, has been my rock for thirty years. She is an excellent travel companion and fellow adventurer, whether in Liverpool, Seattle, New York, Los Angeles, Philadelphia, Siberia, Virgin Gorda, or the French Riviera. Diane deserves a full-scale silver replica of Trinity Church for patiently listening to every last iota of antique skyscraper trivia and helping me to figure out what was worth sharing with you. I told her once I'd write us out of this. I hope I finally kept that promise.

Bibliography

Research for this book relies on newspaper archives, building surveys for the National Register of Historic Places, and extensive online research, as well as the following works and journal articles:

Aliata, Fernando. "La Cantera de la Historia: Mario Palanti y la Construcción de Una Poética Ecléctica en la Argentina." *Cuadernos de Historia del IAA*, vol. 8 (June 1997).

Ambrose, Stephen. *Nothing Like It in the World: The Men Who Built the Transcontinental Railroad, 1863-1869.* Simon & Schuster, 2001.

Aronoff, Jason. "Hascal L. Taylor: The Man Who Commissioned Adler & Sullivan's Buffalo Building." *Western New York Heritage*, vol. 12, no. 1 (Spring 2009).

Avery, Elroy. *A History of Cleveland and Its Environs: The Heart of New Connecticut.* Vol. 2, Lewis Publishing Co., 1918.

Axelrod, Alan. *The Gilded Age, 1876-1912: Overture to the American Century.* Sterling Publishing, 2017.

Bagley, Clarence. *History of Seattle From the Earliest Settlement to the Present Time.* S.J. Clarke Publishing, 1916.

Bagwell, Beth. *Oakland, The Story of a City.* Presidio Press, 1982

Banning , Evelyn. "U.S. Grant, Jr.: A Builder of San Diego." *San Diego Historical Society Quarterly*, vol. 27, no. 1 (Winter 1981).

Barnhouse, Mark. *Daniels and Fisher: Denver's Best Place to Shop.* Arcadia Publishing, 2015.

Bascomb, Neal. Higher: *A Historic Race to the Sky and the Making of a City.* Crown, 2004.

Beard, Patricia. *After the Ball: Gilded Age Secrets, Boardroom Betrayals, and the Party That Ignited the Great Wall Street Scandal of 1905.* Harper Collins, 2003.

Beardsley, Charles. *Hollywood's Master Showman: The Legendary Sid Grauman.* Cornwall Books, 1983.

Berger Elstein, Rochelle. "Adler & Sullivan: The End of the Partnership and Its Aftermath." *Journal of the Illinois State Historical Society,* vol. 98, nos. 1-2 (Spring-Summer 2005).

Betsky, Aaron. *Queer Space: Architecture and Same-Sex Desire.* William Morrow, 1997.

Bliss, Jonathan. *Merchants and Miners in Utah: The Walker Brothers and Their Bank.* Western Epics, 1983.

Bliven, Bruce. *The Wonderful Writing Machine.* Random House, 1954.

Blodgett, Geoffrey. "Cass Gilbert, Architect: Conservative at Bay." *The Journal of American History,* vol. 72, no. 3 (December 1985).

Bluestone, Daniel. *Constructing Chicago.* Yale University Press, 1991.

Bonner, James. *Georgia's Last Frontier: The Development of Carroll County.* University of Georgia Press, 1971.

Boutelle, Sara Holmes. *Julia Morgan, Architect.* Abbeville Press, 1988.

Bradford Laundau, Sarah, and Carl Condit. *Rise of the New York Skyscraper, 1865-1913.* Yale University Press, 1996.

Braly, John. *Memory Pictures, an Autobiography.* Neuner Co., 1912.

Browne, C.A. "The Origins of Sugar Manufacture in America: A Sketch of the History of Sugar Refining in America." *Journal of Chemical Education,* vol. 10, no. 7 (July 1933).

Bruce, H. Addington. *Above the Clouds And Old New York: An Historical Sketch of the Site and a Description of the Many Wonders of the Woolworth Building.* Munder-Thomsen, 1913.

Bruegmann, Robert. *The Architects and the City: Holabird & Roche of Chicago, 1880-1918.* University of Chicago Press, 1997.

Cahan, Richard and Michael Williams. *The Monroe Building: A Chicago Masterpiece Rediscovered.* Master Wings Publishing, 2018.

Caldwell, James. *Recollections of a Life Time.* Baird-Ward Press, 1923.

Carey, Bill. *Fortunes, Fiddles and Fried Chicken: A Nashville Business History.*

Hillsboro Press, 2000.

Christen, Barbara. "Patronage, Process, and Civic Identity: The Development of Cincinnati's Union Central Life Insurance Company Building." *Ohio Valley History*, vol. 9, no. 2 (Summer 2009).

Ciesla, Thomas. "Niels & Mellie Esperson." Unpublished, 2001.

Cox, James. *Journey Through My Years*. Mercer University Press, 2004 (1946).

Crouch, Gregory. *The Bonanza King : John Mackay and the Battle Over the Greatest Riches in the American West*. Scribner, 2018.

Davids Hinton, Diana, and Roger Olien. *Oil in Texas: The Gusher Age, 1895-1945*. University of Texas Press, 2002.

Dietrich, William. *Eminent Pittsburghers: Profiles of the City's Founding Industrialists*. Taylor Trade Publishing, 2011.

Dilts, James. *The World the Trains Made : A Century of Great Railroad Architecture in the United States and Canada*. ForeEdge, 2018.

Dobson, Kevin. *The History of Royal Liver Friendly Society*. Online, 2020.

Duncan, Russell. *Entrepreneur for Equality: Governor Rufus Bullock, Commerce, and Race in Post-Civil War Georgia*. University of Georgia Press, 1994.

Dupré, Judith. *Skyscrapers: A History of the World's Most Extraordinary Buildings*. Black Dog & Leventhal Publishers, 2013.

Elmore, Bartow. *Citizen Coke: The Making of Coca-Cola Capitalism*. New York, 2015.

Equitable Life Assurance Society of the United States. *Henry Baldwin Hyde: A Biographical Sketch*. De Vinne Press, 1901.

Farmer, Silas. *The History of Detroit and Michigan*. Vol. 2, S. Farmer & Co., 1889.

Fedo, David. "Medford Brothers Peter Chardon III and Shepherd Brooks I: The Architectural Revolution in Chicago." *Medford Historical Society & Museum Newsletter*, Winter 2016-17.

Fenske, Gail. *The Skyscraper and the City: The Woolworth Building and the Making of Modern New York*. University of Chicago Press, 2008.

Ferring Shepley, Carol. *Movers and Shakers, Scalawags and Suffragettes: Tales from Bellefontaine Cemetery*. Missouri History Museum, 2008.

Fogelson, Robert. *Downtown: Its Rise and Fall, 1880–1950.* Yale University Press, 2001.

Francis, Daniel. *L.D.: Mayor Louis Taylor and the Rise of Vancouver.* Arsenal Pulp Press, 2004.

Frenzel Jr., Otto. *The City and the Bank, 1865–1965: The Story of Merchants National Bank & Trust Company of Indianapolis.* Benham Press, 1965.

Friedman, Donald, et al. *Ten and Taller, 1874–1900.* Skyscraper Museum exhibit, 2017.

Goldberger, Paul. *The Skyscraper.* Alfred A. Knopf, 1981.

Gray, James. *Business Without Boundary: The Story of General Mills.* University of Minnesota Press, 1954.

Gray, Lee. *From Ascending Rooms to Express Elevators: A History of the Passenger Elevator in the 19th Century.* Elevator World, 2002.

Grunewald, Ehren. "The Origins of New Orleans' Roosevelt Hotel." *Owlcation*, October 2020.

Gustin, Lawrence. *Billy Durant: Creator of General Motors.* Eerdmans, 1973.

Handy, Moses. *The Official Directory of the World's Columbian Exposition.* W.B. Conkey Co., 1893.

Harwood Jr., Herbert. *Invisible Giants: The Empires of Cleveland's Van Sweringen Brothers.* Indiana University Press, 2003.

Hendrick, Burton. "The Story of Life Insurance: The Thirty Years' War" *McClure's Magazine*, vol. 27, no. 5 (September 1906).

Hoffmann, Donald. *Frank Lloyd Wright, Louis Sullivan, and the Skyscraper.* Dover Publications, 1998.

Holian, Timothy. "Adolphus Busch" in *Immigrant Entrepreneurship: German–American Business Biographies, 1720 to the Present, vol. 2, The Emergence of an Industrial Nation, 1840–1893.* German Historical Institute, 2013.

Houchins, John et al. *L.C. Smith: An American Best Quality Sidelock Side by Side Shotgun and Among the World's Most Famous.* Jostens, 2006.

Irish, Sharon. *Cass Gilbert, Architect : Modern Traditionalist.* Monacelli Press, 1999.

James, Henry. *The American Scene.* Chapman & Hall, 1907.

Jefferson, Sam. *Gordon Bennett and the First Yacht Race Across the Atlantic.* Adlard Coles, 2017.

Jennings, Jan. *Cheap and Tasteful Dwellings: Design Competitions and the Convenient Interior, 1879-1909.* University of Tennessee Press, 2005.

Johnson, Charlie. *The Daniels & Fisher Tower: A Presence of the Past.* Tower Press, 1977.

Kidney, Walter. *Pittsburgh's Landmark Architecture : The Historic Buildings of Pittsburgh and Allegheny County.* Pittsburgh History & Landmarks Foundation, 1997.

Korom, Joseph. *The American Skyscraper, 1850-1940: A Celebration of Height.* Branden Books, 2008.

Landau, Sarah. *George B. Post, Architect: Picturesque Designer and Determined Realist.* Monacelli Press, 1998.

Larson, Erik. *The Devil in the White City.* Vintage Books, 2003.

Lenard, Tom, dir. *Horace: The Bridge Builder King.* Auburn University, 1996.

Luhrs, George. *The Geo. H.N. Luhrs Family in Phoenix and Arizona, 1847-1984.* J.S. Crane, 1988.

Luke, Bob. *Bromo-Seltzer King: The Opulent Life of Captain Isaac "Ike" Emerson, 1859-1931.* McFarland, 2019.

Mauldin Cottrell, Debbie. "Mellie Keenan Esperson" in *Handbook of Texas Online.* Texas State Historical Association, 2020.

Maxwell Elebash, Camille. "The Jemison Mansion Family Histories," *Alabama Heritage,* no. 26 (Fall 1992).

McCarthy, James. *Peacock Alley: The Romance of the Waldorf-Astoria.* Harper, 1931.

McDowall, Duncan. *Quick to the Frontier: Canada's Royal Bank.* McClelland & Stewart, 1993.

McNeill, Karen. "Women Who Build: Julia Morgan and Women's Institutions." *California History,* vol. 89, no. 3 (2012).

Merwood-Salisbury, Joanna. *Chicago 1890: The Skyscraper and the Modern City.* University of Chicago Press, 2009.

Mitchell, Margaret. *Gone With the Wind.* Macmillan, 1936.

Monroe, Harriet. *John Wellborn Root: A Study of His Life and Work.* Riverside

Press, 1896.

Moudry, Roberta, ed. *The American Skyscraper: Cultural Histories.* Cambridge University Press, 2005.

Murphy, Kevin, and Lisa Reilly, eds. *Skyscraper Gothic: Medieval Style and Modernist Buildings.* Charlottesville, 2017

Murray, Jackson. *Memories of Jackson Murray, Former Slave of the Hennen Family Written When He Was 92 Years of Age.* Historic New Orleans Collection, 1908.

Nasaw, David. *The Chief: The Life of William Randolph Hearst.* Houghton Mifflin, 2000.

Neumann, Dietrich. "A Skyscraper for Mussolini." *AA Files,* vol. 68 (2014).

O'Connor, Richard. "The Wayward Commodore." *American Heritage,* vol. 25, no. 4 (June 1974).

Owen, Nancy. "Marketing Rookwood Pottery: Culture and Consumption, 1883-1913." *Studies in the Decorative Arts,* vol. 4, no. 2 (Spring-Summer 1997).

Pacini, Lauren. *Honoring their Memory: Levi T. Schofield, Cleveland's Monumental Architect and Sculptor.* Artography Press, 2019.

Pajot, Dennis. *Building Milwaukee City Hall: The Political, Legal and Construction Battles.* McFarland & Co., 2013.

Peet, Gerard. "The Origin of the Skyscraper." *Council on Tall Buildings and Urban Habitat Journal,* issue I, 2011.

Pendergrast, Mark. *For God, Country, and Coca-Cola: The Definitive History of the Great American Soft Drink and the Company That Makes It.* Basic Books, 2013.

Pinckard, Jane. *Lest We Forget: The Open Gates, The George Sealy Residence.* J. & R. Pinckard, 1988.

Ponder, Melinda. *Katharine Lee Bates: From Sea to Shining Sea.* Windy City Publishers, 2017.

Pridmore, Jay. *The Reliance Building: A Building Book from the Chicago Architecture Foundation.* Pomegranate Communications, 2003.

Report of the Heights of Buildings Commission to the Committee on the Height, Size and Arrangement of Buildings of the Board of Estimate and Apportionment of the City of New York. 1913.

Saliga, Pauline. *The Sky's The Limit: A Century of Chicago Skyscrapers*. Rizzoli, 1990.

Salt Lake Tribune. "Joseph Robinson Walker" in *Sketches of the Inter-Mountain States: Together with Biographies of Many Prominent and Progressive Citizens Who Have Helped in the Development and History-Making of this Marvelous Region, 1847-1909*. Salt Lake Tribune, 1909.

Schaffer, Kristen. *Daniel H. Burnham: Visionary Architect and Planner*. Rizzoli, 2003.

Schwarz, Judith. "Yellow Clover: Katharine Lee Bates and Katharine Coman." *Frontiers: A Journal of Women Studies*, vol. 4, no. 1 (Spring 1979).

Seidel, Emil. *Autobiography of Emil Seidel*. Unpublished, 1944.

Shutter, Marion, ed. *History of Minneapolis: Gateway to the Northwest*. S.J. Clarke Publishing, 1923.

Siry, Joseph. "Adler and Sullivan's Guaranty Building in Buffalo." *Journal of the Society of Architectural Historians*, vol. 55, no. 1 (March 1996).

Sloan, Alfred. *My Years with General Motors*. Doubleday, 1990 (1963).

Smith, Michael. *Designing Detroit : Wirt Rowland and the Rise of Modern American Architecture*. Wayne State University Press, 2017.

Smith, Richard. *The Colonel: The Life and Legend of Robert McCormick*. Northwestern University Press, 2003.

Solomonson, Katherine. *The Chicago Tribune Tower Competition: Skyscraper Design and Cultural Change in the 1920s*. University of Chicago Press, 2003.

Sparberg Alexiou, Alice. *The Flatiron: The New York Landmark and the Incomparable City That Arose With It*. Thomas Dunne, 2010.

Standiford, Les. *Meet You in Hell: Andrew Carnegie, Henry Clay Frick, and the Bitter Partnership That Changed America*. Crown, 2006.

Steffens, Lincoln. *The Shame of the Cities*. McClure, Phillips & Co., 1904.

Stevens, Otheman, ed. "Frank Kanning Mott" in *Press Reference Library: Notables of the Southwest, Being the Portraits and Biographies of Progressive Men of the Southwest, Who Have Helped in the Development and History Making of this Wonderful Country*. Los Angeles Examiner, 1912.

Stocking, William, and Gordon Miller. *The City of Detroit, Michigan, 1701-1922*. Vol. 3, 1922.

Stone, Irving. *They Also Ran: The Story of the Men Who Were Defeated for the Presidency.* Doubleday, Doran & Co., 1944.

Stover, John. *History of the Baltimore and Ohio Railroad.* Purdue University Press, 1995

Sullivan, Louis. "The Tall Office Building Artistically Considered." *Lippincott's Monthly Magazine*, vol. 339 (March 1896).

Sullivan, Louis. *The Autobiography of An Idea.* Dover Publications, 1956 (1924).

Tarbell, Ida. *The History of the Standard Oil Company.* McClure, Phillips & Co., 1904.

Thorne, Robert, ed. *Structural Iron and Steel, 1850-1900.* Routledge, 2000.

U.S. Geological Survey. *The San Francisco Earthquake and Fire of April 18, 1906, and their Effects on Structures and Structural Materials.* Government Printing Office, 1907.

Uhry Abrams, Ann. *Formula for Fortune: How Asa Candler Discovered Coca-Cola and Turned It Into the Wealth His Children Enjoyed.* iUniverse, 2012.

Union Central Life Insurance Company. *Jesse Redman Clark, 1854-1921.* Private, 1921.

Van der Schuit, J.J. "100 Jaar Het Witte Huis: Opkomst en Ondergang van de Heren Van der Schuit." *Effe Lùstere*, vols. 1-2, 1999.

Vitiello, Domenic. "Monopolizing the Metropolis: Gilded Age Growth Machines and Power in American Urbanization." *Planning Perspectives*, vol. 28, no. 1 (2013).

Watts, Leslie. "George Sealy II" in *Handbook of Texas Online.* Texas State Historical Association, 2020.

Weisman, Winston. "New York and the Problem of the First Skyscraper." *Journal of the Society of Architectural Historians*, vol. 12, no. 1 (March 1953).

Weisman, Winston. "Philadelphia Functionalism and Sullivan." *Journal of the Society of Architectural Historians*, vol. 20, no. 1 (March 1961).

Willis, Carol. *Form Follows Finance: Skyscrapers and Skylines in New York and Chicago.* Princeton Architectural Press, 1995.

Winkler, John. *Five and Ten: The Fabulous Life of F. W. Woolworth.* McBride & Co., 1940.

Wiseman, Carter. "The Rise of the Skyscraper and the Fall of Louis Sullivan." *American Heritage*, vol. 49, no. 1 (February/March 1998).

Woolworth, F.W., Co. *The Cathedral of Commerce: The Highest Building in the World*. Munder-Thomsen, 1916.

Young, Andrew. *History of Chautauqua County, New York*. Dalcassian Publishing, 1875.

Index

About the Author

Mark Houser is a frequent writer and speaker on historic topics and recently won the Press Club of Western Pennsylvania Golden Quill Award for magazine journalism on history and culture. Houser is director of news and information at Robert Morris University, and has worked with foreign students to create an audio walking tour of Pittsburgh in eleven languages. He spent fifteen years at the *Pittsburgh Tribune-Review*, where his work won national and international awards and led to appearances on CNN, FOX, and NPR. As a coordinator and former transatlantic fellow with the German Marshall Fund of the United States, he has arranged itineraries for more than one hundred European professionals visiting Pittsburgh, including a young Emmanuel Macron before he became president of France. Mark and his wife, Diane, live in suburban Pittsburgh and love to travel. This is his first book.

BOOK MARK *to speak at your conference, corporate function, or private event!*
Go to **HouserTalks.com** *to learn more and inquire about arrangements.*